The Relationship
Doctor's
Prescription
FOR$_x$

Building
Your Child's
Self-Image

Dr. David Hawkins

HARVEST HOUSE PUBLISHERS

EUGENE, OREGON

THE RELATIONSHIP DOCTOR'S PRESCRIPTION FOR BUILDING YOUR CHILD'S SELF-IMAGE
Copyright © 2007 by David Hawkins
Published by Harvest House Publishers
Eugene, Oregon 97402
www.harvesthousepublishers.com

Library of Congress Cataloging-in-Publication Data
Hawkins, David, 1951-
The relationship doctor's prescription for building your child's self-image / David Hawkins.
   p. cm.
Includes bibliographical references.
  ISBN-13: 978-0-7369-1951-7 (pbk.)
  ISBN-10: 0-7369-1951-1
  1. Self-perception—Religious aspects—Christianity. 2. Self-perception in children. 3. Parenting—Religious aspects—Christianity. 4. Child rearing—Religious aspects—Christianity. I. Title.
  BV4598.25.H39 2007
  248.8'45—dc22
                                                        2006030637

Printed in the United States of America

07 08 09 10 11 12 13 14 15 / BP-CF / 10 9 8 7 6 5 4 3 2 1

Contents

A Note from the Author

Several years ago, while in a particularly creative mood, I took a pottery class. Pottery 101. I dreamed of making goblets and ceramic bowls. How tough could that be? If my Michelangelesque skills were lacking, perhaps the new electric pottery wheels would do the work for me. All I had to do was show up, grab the clay, plunk myself in front of the spinning wheel, and *voilà!*—a gorgeous bowl would appear.

As you might guess, this was not how events developed. My first attempt at making a bowl was arduous. Clay flew off the spinning wheel in every direction. I picked pieces of clay off my shirt and out of my eyes with no delightful product to show for my efforts. However, my time was not wasted. I had entered the experience hoping to create something, Instead, I came out of it being someone.

As our teacher, Carl Jenkins, a former Lutheran pastor, methodically sculpted a magnificent bowl, he talked about the scriptural theme of creating something out of clay. He taught us that with our talents and gifts—large and small—we can create something new and wonderful.

Carl reminded us that God was the first potter. He created man out of the dust of the ground and breathed into him the breath of life (Genesis 2:7). God did a far better job with the bit of clay He had than I did with mine. I couldn't make a recognizable ceramic bowl; God created a wonderful human being. God not only formed Adam, He also formed each of us. The prophet Isaiah referred to God as "he who made you, who formed you in the womb, and who will help you" (Isaiah 44:2).

"Go down to the potter's house," the Lord said to the prophet

Jeremiah, "and there I will give you my message…Like clay in the hand of the potter, so you are in my hand" (Jeremiah 18:2,6). God appreciated the illustration of the potter and the clay. He created us in His image, and He is continually in the process of molding us more and more into His likeness. He is a potter, and therefore we are all potters in one way or another. God has graced us with the gift of being cocreators with Him, and the act of creation goes on.

As a parent, you have one of the greatest opportunities to co-create with God. He is still in the creative business and invites us to join Him in that creative process. You have the opportunity to help build your child's self-image. You participated, of course, in the formation of your child, but that is only the beginning. After conception and birth, the creative process continues. The opportunity is enormous and the responsibility is great.

In *The Relationship Doctor's Prescription for Building Your Child's Self-Image* you will learn about normal child development. You will understand and appreciate God's plan for raising children and your responsibility as a parent. You will understand what the term *self-image* means. You will read about the importance of self-image and what you can do as a parent to build your child's healthy self-image.

You will also learn what can go wrong and how abuse, neglect, and harsh and critical environments can damage a child's self-image. What symptoms in a child indicate something might be going wrong? What traits can you expect from a child with a healthy self-image? You will learn strategies for creating healthy friendships and making the most of peer interactions. Most important, you will learn how to be a potter, creating the best world in which your child can thrive and become the person God has intended him or her to be.

Let's move ahead now and learn about children and how you can be instrumental in building their positive self-image—one that will carry them all through life.

1

Cocreating
Our Child's Self-Image

I distinctly remember the birth experience of my two sons, Joshua and Tyson. Their mother and I had prepared extensively for the experience. We read up on the latest, greatest techniques for birthing children, attempting to minimize birth's trauma. Thankfully, our sons were born healthy and strong. I remember looking at these two gooey bundles of flesh and thinking, *Lord, what now? They are so helpless, so demanding, so needy. Am I supposed to dedicate the next 18 years of my life to meeting all of their needs? Did I really know what I was getting into when I signed up for this project?* Being a parent has been a sobering and exciting experience.

Raising a child, or children, is perhaps the most difficult thing you will ever do. As you were growing up, you probably had grand ideas of being a perfect parent and having wonderful, perfect children. Your little girl would be athletic in high school, going on to compete in the Olympics. She would then enter college and become a powerful attorney. Your son would letter in three sports, complete college, and become a successful businessman. Perhaps your goals were even loftier—your child would become the next renowned rocket scientist or possibly run for senator of the United States.

As you dreamed large dreams for your children, you spared no expense. You determined to buy them nice clothes and new toys and to decorate their rooms so they would be in a stimulating environment. You vowed to take them to church for their spiritual development. You were ready for your first child.

Certainly, nothing is wrong with these dreams. In fact, dreaming about your children's future and their possibilities is exciting. But did you consider the primary building blocks to their success? You undoubtedly thought about providing them with a secure and loving home, and that is surely a wonderful beginning. But did you think beyond that, to the specific tools they would need to be successful adults? This book will help you understand one of the most crucial character traits necessary for successful adulthood: a strong and healthy self-image.

But what exactly is self-image? We throw out terms like *healthy self-esteem* or *positive self-image* without knowing exactly what we are talking about. Let's get that confusion cleared up.

I grew up in a family of seven people. As a middle child, I distinctly remember the feeling of having two older siblings and two younger. Someone was always telling me what to do—my older brother or sister—and I always had someone to boss around—my two younger sisters. I had two strong, confident parents who guided me along my personal journey of developing a positive self-image. Each of these people helped define this thing called *David*.

My family of origin was the place where I learned about who I was—my identity, my self-image. I learned about my core sense of self. This was where I learned a number of critical building blocks that shaped my positive self-image. In the Hawkins family and the neighborhood surrounding our family home, I learned these things about myself:

- I am loved and accepted.
- I am capable of learning new things.
- I am able to safely explore my world.
- I am capable athletically.
- I am welcome in my family, my church, and my neighborhood.
- I am ambitious and determined.
- I am a leader.
- I have positive physical attributes.
- I am able to assert myself to get my needs met.
- I am a spiritual person.

All of these factors, woven integrally together, were part of my developing self-image—my identity and positive view of myself.

My parents actively reinforced these aspects of my identity. Had they not had a clear and constructive plan of parenting, I could have easily developed a different picture of myself:

- I am unlovable and unacceptable.
- I am incapable of learning new things.
- I am not safe in exploring the world, or the world is an unsafe and dangerous place.
- I am inept and awkward physically.
- I am unwelcome in my family, church, and neighborhood.
- I am lazy and unmotivated.
- I am ugly.
- I am unable or forbidden to ask for what I need.
- I have no spirituality.

Consider the amazing difference between these two lists. Consider the remarkable impact these two different mind-sets can have on a child's outcome. These lists clearly show that parents, friends, schoolmates, and other influences can make an enormous difference in an individual's self-image. Many destructive events can take place in a child's life, including parental divorce, abandonment, and abuse, and these can drastically alter a child's self-image. But we will discover that we can deal with even these events in an effective manner. Jean Illsley Clark says this in her book *Self-Esteem: A Family Affair:*

> Positive self-esteem is important because when people experience it, they feel good and look good, they are effective and productive, and they respond to other people and themselves in healthy, positive, growing ways. People who have positive self-esteem know that they are lovable and capable, and they care about themselves and other people. They do not have to build themselves up by tearing other people down or by patronizing less competent people.[1]

Christians have been confused and ruffled by issues of self-esteem or self-image. I have found in my counseling experience that many are quick to ridicule any notions surrounding self-image. They believe that our self-image is so completely rooted in who we are as Christians that we should never be concerned with teaching self-image concepts. I certainly agree that our faith is the foundation of our identity, but that's not the end of the story.

Having clarified what self-image is, let's clarify what it is not:

- self-centeredness
- acting superior
- being a braggart
- pushing one's agenda

The Scriptures clearly say we are not to think of ourselves more highly that we ought to think (Romans 12:3). But they do not say we are to see ourselves as incapable, unlovable, or unacceptable. As in all things, balance is the key.

Is Self-Image That Important?

What is so important about self-image? Why a book devoted to the topic? Some believe all this talk about children's self-image, and the promotion of self-esteem, simply promotes self-centered, narcissistic, and indulged brats.

Betsy Hart, in her book *It Takes a Parent*, takes to task those who say developing a child's self-esteem is a parent's most important task. "What about the idea of raising children who are compassionate and who esteem others?...'Other esteem' just doesn't seem to have much of a following in the parenting culture—or in the culture in general." Ms. Hart lambastes those who promote boundless promotion of the self. "The self-esteem movement is hanging on tight in the parenting culture. This despite the fact that there is no evidence to show that it's the cure for all the ills it claims to be."[2]

While Ms. Hart's passions are understandable, she makes some key mistakes in her thinking. She emphasizes the error of praising little Johnny for whatever he does, however he does it. I do not believe we should heap praise on our children regardless of their behavior. Quite the opposite. I believe we should encourage children for behavior that shows effort in their tasks, values that promote spiritual and emotional well-being for themselves and others, and compassion for family, friends, and society.

Ms. Hart also comes dangerously close to making another grievous error. She finds no evidence showing that healthy self-esteem is a cure for anything. But in fact, a healthy self-image, which incorporates self-esteem, is linked to many emotional and social benefits. Bob Murray and Alicia Fortinberry, in their book *Raising an Optimistic Child*, state, "Lack of true self-esteem and a sense of competence are underlying causes of depression, and a threat to these can trigger a depressive episode."[3]

Murray and Fortinberry cite the American Academy of Pediatrics, which shows that the opposite of promoting self-esteem, "belittling, degrading, or ridiculing a child, is a major cause of depression."[4]

The evidence powerfully demonstrates that promoting a healthy self-image within a child is worth our greatest efforts.

The Crucial Ingredient

Let me up the ante. Promoting our child's self-image is not only worthy of our best efforts, it is absolutely crucial. A healthy self-image is perhaps the most important component of a person's character.

Dorothy Corkille Briggs, author of *Your Child's Self-Esteem*, believes that as parents we must do more than help our children avoid nervous breakdowns, fall into addictions to drugs and alcohol, or lapse into delinquency. These goals are important, but they are not enough. Briggs says that we must dedicate ourselves to helping our children develop "a firm and wholehearted belief in themselves"— another excellent definition of self-image. To that end she says children have two basic needs:

First, to develop a belief that they are lovable. Briggs believes children need to have an unwavering belief that they matter and have value because they exist.

Second, to develop a belief that they are worthwhile. Children must believe they can handle themselves and their environment with competence. They need the conviction that they have something to offer others.

Briggs says we can meet many other needs for safety, security, and stimulation, but if we do not create a climate within the home and family relationships that helps children develop these two beliefs, trouble will certainly follow.

> Meeting these needs is as essential for emotional well-being as oxygen is for physical survival. Each of us, after all, is our own lifelong roommate. The one person you cannot avoid, no matter how hard you try, is you. And so it is with your child. He lives most intimately with himself, and it is of utmost importance for his optimal growth, as well as a meaningful and

> rewarding life, that he respect himself…It is the child's
> feeling about being loved or unloved that affects how
> he will develop.[5]

Is this thing called *self-image* that important, you wonder? If I love my child, but somehow he or she doesn't feel or integrate my love, will damage result? Yes. So much of life beyond childhood hangs on the wings of a strong and healthy respect for self—self-image.

Healthy Self-Image or Noisy Conceit

After reading this you may wonder if I am pandering to New Age gurus who would have us believe the power lies within, who say we are the masters of our own destiny, that we can do all things through our own hidden potential.

No, I am not promoting an attitude that says, "I can run the world if you will only listen to me." I am not encouraging parents to place little Tommy and Susie on the throne of their own lives. Far from it. Rather, I am talking about the importance of a healthy and balanced self-image—not an overstuffed ego. I am talking about a quiet sense of self-respect, not noisy conceit. Arrogance is an aberration of self-respect, a strong self-concept gone askew. It is actually whitewash to cover low self-esteem.

When children have a healthy respect for themselves, they have a healthy respect for others. They know and are convinced that they matter, but they also know that others matter as well. In fact, to treat others with dignity and respect is one of the hallmarks of a healthy self-image.

So don't worry that we are heading down a slippery slope to a godless humanism. We will not promote the worth of an individual above others or above God. We will promote a balanced perspective, completely in line with scriptural teachings.

Let's now look into the life of a typical child and see how self-image plays a critical role in development.

2

The Life of a Child

Timmy James was a rough-and-tumble, mischievous child of nine, with curly blond hair bursting from the sides and back of the ball cap turned backward on his head. He was a curious child, willing to find clever ways of keeping himself entertained. Whenever he joined a couple of like-minded youngsters, he was likely to find a good time—or trouble.

Timmy was delighted that his parents had chosen to live in a housing development with lots of children. Some of the children were well-behaved and cautious; others were daring and creative, like his best friends, Tommy and Craig.

When Timmy wasn't attending school, he was riding his bike with Tommy or Craig, who lived less than two minutes away. They were like Timmy in many ways but a bit more rebellious. They tended to be labeled *troublemakers* at school and frequently were in the principal's office for talking back to teachers or erupting with anger when someone teased them. When teachers confronted them about their behavior in school, they made excuses, got angry, or complained that others disliked them.

During their better times, Timmy and his friends were busy building ramps to use as jumps for their bikes or skateboards. When they weren't engaged in daredevil enterprises, they often tried to outperform one another on a video game. They played PlayStation, Xbox, or one of the other latest, greatest video games.

Timmy's teachers said he was "a borderline kid," meaning he seemed to have one foot in positive activities and one foot in trouble. He was a child with a mixed temperament. He was capable of having fun when with his friends, but his mood quickly shifted at home, where he had the misfortune of living amid a variety of family problems. Here, living with two working parents, one older sibling, and one younger sibling, he often had a vague feeling of sadness. He never came out and said that he was sad, of course. But his behavior hinted at underlying trouble.

Timmy's dad was a long-haul truck driver who was gone four or five days a week and home most weekends. Timmy ached to see his dad more often. He never voiced his frustration, however, because he knew his dad was a hard worker and needed to drive his truck to pay their bills. Timmy's mother worked as a secretary in a medical clinic. She too was gone a lot. Timmy had asked his mom once if she could stay home more often to be with him, but she scolded him and told him he should be happy she worked to give their family the extra things they enjoyed.

Timmy came to accept his father's absence and his mother working long hours. During their time away, he played outside with the other children who ran the streets. Before long, he began having problems at school. His extra energy, which the school psychologist suspected might be attention deficit hyperactivity disorder, tended to create problems in the classroom. He didn't like the classroom experience and was easily distracted, and that created a challenging combination. He had trouble getting schoolwork done, was often out of his seat, and spent more than his share of time in detention.

Timmy's problems multiplied. His teachers began sending reports home to his parents indicating their concern. As you might guess, Timmy's parents did not appreciate having to deal with his problems. They struggled to cope with their own problems and weren't ready to take on more. They were impatient with his situation and told him he had better straighten up or he would be in worse trouble at home—which is exactly what happened.

Timmy is caught in a whirlpool of problems. He is falling behind academically, he's starting to really dislike school, and he's becoming known as a troublemaker. His parents are frustrated and don't have the extra energy to spend supervising his schooling. Feeling even lonelier, Timmy seems sadder and angrier every day. His world is flying out of control. He wonders if he is the bad child his parents say he is, the troublemaker his classmates and teachers believe him to be.

Out of desperation, Timmy's mother called my office for an appointment.

"What is wrong with my child?" she asked during her first visit. Staring angrily at Timmy, who busied himself with Legos, she said, "I don't have the patience for him. He has all this energy, and instead of using it for good, he seems to want to get into trouble. I can't understand it. It's like he enjoys being a troublemaker."

"First of all, Mrs. James, I don't think Timmy wants to be a troublemaker. Kids don't grow up wanting to be troublemakers. Their behavior is usually a symptom of something else happening in their life. Trouble, as you call it, is a symptom of something deeper, and we have to be detectives to find it."

I turned and looked at Timmy and smiled. I noticed he had been watching us the entire time.

"I'll bet you lay awake at night thinking of ways to make your teachers upset, right?"

"No," Timmy said, breaking into a small grin. He then looked at his mother, anxiously. "I hate being in trouble."

"I don't think being in trouble is any fun," I said. "And being teased by other kids is sure no fun. We'll have to figure this thing out together. We'll find out what Timmy needs to be successful at school, with his friends, and at home. He can do it, and we'll help him get there."

I encouraged Timmy's mother to bring his father with her to another appointment, when we could explore the family dynamics and possible medical issues that might be causing the problems. We briefly explored how Timmy's behavior probably stemmed from issues related to his self-image, and we discussed how Timmy's behavior was impacting the family. We agreed to look deeper into the problems to arrive at an accurate diagnosis, which would help us move to a remedy and helpful course of action.

An Interplay of Factors

After Timmy and his mother left my office, I reflected about their situation. I wondered what it was like to live in Timmy's world. What was it like to wonder when your parents would come home in the evening and in what mood? What was it like to feel empty, longing for a family to come home to, imagining a warm dinner with parents and siblings? How did Timmy feel about being labeled a troublemaker? Did he feel warm and loved, or did he fall asleep at night feeling a vague sense of rejection?

A quick glance at Timmy's life reveals a mixture of events and circumstances that undoubtedly impact his sense of self—some innate traits, some a product of his environment. Let's summarize the more obvious ones:

- His father is often absent from the home.

- His mother works long hours.

- He has many hours of unsupervised activity.

- He may have a medical/psychological condition known as attention deficit hyperactivity disorder.

- He has learning difficulties.

- He plays with other children who have similar problems.
- He is labeled a troublemaker.
- His parents are intolerant of his problems.

Each of these factors influences the others, multiplying their effect. A child's behavior, or self-image, is rarely the result of one event or problem. Rather, self-image is developed by the interplay of factors. In this case, Timmy's self-image was developing in a negative direction, and his outlook would improve only if many of these factors changed.

Indicators of a Healthy Sense of Self

Timmy James is in trouble. His family is in trouble. Fortunately, they are seeking help relatively early, and together we can begin to turn things around. How do we know Timmy is in trouble? How do we know his problems might be related to self-image?

Barbara Coloroso has written a delightful book titled *Kids Are Worth It*. In it she describes articulately what exactly we are looking for when we seek to enhance and develop our child's self-image. Her insights are powerful, and I invite you to review these qualities as indicators of a healthy self-image. Note where your child excels and where he or she might have difficulties.

- *Acts out of a sense of conviction.* Do your child's actions stem from clear, healthy values, and is she willing to hold to those values in the face of disapproval?

- *Takes initiative—does not wait for an adult to approve or affirm.* Does your child make his own decisions and act on them?

- *Has an internally defined sense of self. Lives consciously and purposely.* Has your child taken the time to decide

who she is, what she values, and how she is different
from you?

- *Accepts responsibility for decisions, choices, and mistakes.*
  Does your child make excuses for his mistakes, or does
  he take responsibility for them? Is he able to listen to
  constructive criticism?

- *Accepts the past, learns from it, and lets it go.* Does your
  child accept her mistakes and learn from them? Does
  she beat herself up for her failures?

- *Is optimistic, has realistic expectations, and maintains a
  positive outlook.* Is your child generally optimistic? Does
  he recognize a reciprocal relationship between optimism
  and a healthy self-image?

- *Feels empowered and self-directed.* Does your child have
  a sense that she can tackle most problems and move forward with a can-do attitude?

- *Celebrates and cherishes success.* Is your child able to sit
  back and smile about his accomplishments?

- *Knows her abilities, is willing to share, and is open to others'
  ideas.* Does your child have a realistic self-appraisal? Is
  she willing to champion herself and others?

- *Is willing to take risks.* Is your child willing to press into
  change for the purpose of growth?

- *Is open to constructive criticism as well as compliments
  and measures both in relation to core identity.* Is your
  child able to listen to feedback about his behavior, both
  positive and negative, and evaluate it in terms of who he
  is and what he wants to accomplish in his life?

- *Possesses personal integrity and self-respect.* Does your child
  have a set of ethics and morals that guides her life?

- *Is confident and self-expressive; listens to internal signals and intuition.* Is your child able to share his feelings and thoughts with others? Does he trust that his beliefs may be based on hunches and ideas that are very personal to him?

- *Explores and goes beyond conventional ideas—is creative.* Is your child able to think and act outside convention? Is she able to see things in new ways, and is she willing to explore her unique creativity?

- *Is playful; doesn't need for everything to have a purpose.* Does your child have the capacity to be wild, crazy, and fun? Is he able to laugh at himself and not take life too seriously?

- *Is altruistic, ethical, and compassionate; attends to others' feelings and points of view.* Does your child have a clear sense of self? Is she secure and able to operate outside of her own needs and desires at times, listening and attending to the concerns of others?

- *Examines values before accepting them as his own.* Does your child consider "truths" he hears? Has he reached a stage where he can hear other points of view and finally decide if he can own them?[1]

Consider this list of traits. Take a few moments and evaluate your child in terms of these attributes. In what areas is your child strong? What are her strengths you can reinforce? Don't be discouraged if she has areas of concern. If you discovered some weaknesses, you probably already have some ideas about what needs to be changed.

We will talk about ways to bolster your child's self-image. Can you set some goals to begin working on those areas of concern? We will talk more about addressing these concerns and building on positive attributes as we move together through this book. We will explore them in the context of different families and help you explore them in your family as well.

3

How Children
Are Made

There can be no better place to begin talking about children like Timmy, or families like the Jameses, than to understand God's heart on the matter. After all, if we really want to start where it all began, we must start at the beginning—God's beginning.

In the beginning God created the heavens and the earth. But He didn't stop there. He created man, and then, understanding that it was not good for man to be alone, He created woman. Well, you know the rest of the story. He instructed Adam and Eve to be fruitful and multiply and to have dominion over the earth (Genesis 1:28). Clearly, God had families in mind when He created the universe. Children were part of this natural order.

Families were clearly in the heart of God at the beginning of creation. Moving through the Old Testament we see the historical message of salvation woven through the story of families. Consider Abraham and Sarah and their desire to have children. Abraham was moved with distress when he confronted God: "O Sovereign LORD, what can you give me since I remain childless?" He had no heir to pass his estate to. But God knew a miracle was about to happen— Abraham was going to be a father and grandfather many times over.

"Look up at the heavens and count the stars—if indeed you can count them...So shall your offspring be" (Genesis 15:2-5). This was no small miracle given Abraham and Sarah's advanced ages.

Consider Jacob and the saga of working years to obtain Laban's daughter Rachel as his wife—and their drama of being unable to have children. Through deception Leah became Jacob's first wife, and he had children by her. His beloved Rachel was his second wife, and she was barren. After years of family conflict, fraught with jealousy and infighting between Rachel and Leah, Rachel was finally honored. "Then God remembered Rachel; he listened to her and opened her womb. She became pregnant and gave birth to a son and said, 'God has taken away my disgrace'" (Genesis 30:22).

As we move into the New Testament, we witness the birth and development of Jesus Himself. The Gospels are rather silent about his early childhood, but Luke gives us a notation that we should not overlook. Jesus' parents traveled to Jerusalem for the Feast of the Passover and took 12-year-old Jesus with them. Jesus' parents began the journey home, but Jesus stayed behind without their awareness. At some point they realized Jesus was not in their entourage and finally found Him in the temple courts.

> When his parents saw him, they were astonished. His mother said to him, "Son, why have you treated us like this? Your father and I have been anxiously searching for you."
>
> "Why were you searching for me?" he asked. "Didn't you know I had to be in my Father's house?" But they did not understand what he was saying to them.
>
> Then he went to Nazareth with them and was obedient to them. But his mother treasured all these things in her heart. *And Jesus grew in wisdom and stature, and in favor with God and men* (Luke 2:48-52).

We see that Jesus was a normal youth in many ways. Though certainly God, He was also a normal boy who would mature and grow. Sensing His call to obey the Father, He stayed in Jerusalem. His parents reacted as many of us would today—with anxiety about their missing son. After they scolded Jesus, we see that He was obedient to them.

Luke points out three areas of growth in Jesus:

- wisdom (spiritual insight)
- stature (physical size)
- favor with God and man

Jesus gained favor with people. His parents raised Him, and God blessed Him, in such a way that people were attracted to Him. He was also favored by God, His heavenly Father.

As Jesus matures we see Him as a sensitive and caring young man. We read the touching story of Jesus correcting His disciples, who were hindering the children from coming to Him (Matthew 19:14). How many paintings show Jesus holding a little child? Jesus obviously adored little children. We also know of the oft-quoted Scripture imploring us to "become like little children" as we approach Him (Matthew 18:3). I interpret that passage to mean that we are to lay down our self-righteous, self-important attitudes and posturing and simply approach Him with childlike honesty.

Children have a high place in Jesus' heart and teachings, and this sets the stage for how we should view them. He gave them a place of honor, and so should we. I believe Jesus approves of the importance we place on children's self-image.

Our Historical View of Children

In contrast to Jesus' words and actions, for many years our society has treated children as if they were second-class citizens. They are small, helpless, immature human beings, and therefore we sometimes treat them any way we choose. For years, in many cultures, children were abused, treated harshly, and punished severely for even the slightest misbehavior. We are embarrassed to admit that we once worked children 14 hours a day for no wage. We have sent children to boarding schools for "incorrigibility," which often meant any form of misbehavior.

We are well beyond treating our children as chattel, you might think. Sadly, this is simply not the case. Every day state agencies receive calls from indignant neighbors, indicating a child is being left alone while her parent slips away to smoke marijuana or escapes into a hypnotic sleep after taking a hit of cocaine. Self-indulgent parents party as if they have no small and helpless children who are totally reliant upon them for physical sustenance. These are absentee parents who are self-involved, unable to provide the emotional and spiritual supervision needed for building a child's healthy self-image.

The abhorrent neglect associated with drug and alcohol abuse is not the only culprit harming our children. Every day teachers see eerily frightening and unexplainable marks on children's bodies, which physicians determine to be the bruises of an angry parent. Too often our morgues are filled with children who have fatally suffered from shaken baby syndrome.

I was asked recently to perform an evaluation on a mother who was seen cursing at her two-year-old child in the emergency room of a local hospital. Her child was being treated for a raging fever that had been neglected for days. The mother, 18 years old, terribly immature and insensitive, saw nothing wrong with her actions and even defended them.

"She was screaming her head off and wouldn't shut up. So I told her to knock that crap off. What's so bad about that?"

"Well," I said firmly, "what's so bad about that is that the child was screaming because of the pain she was feeling from her fever, the one she had for hours. You didn't take care of your child's fever, so she was naturally screaming because she was in pain."

"So I lost my temper," the mother said defensively. "I don't think the state needed to be called."

But the appropriate state agency was called, as routinely happens several times a day in cities all across America. They receive these calls because far too many parents take poor care of their children. Kids suffer needlessly, and our foster care system is overburdened as a result. Far too many parents directly or indirectly harm their children, and children are the needless victims.

An All-American Family

What does all of that troubling history have to do with you and me? Perhaps very little, other than to give you a perspective of the way many people in our society treat our children. However, many children's neglect and abandonment do not come to the attention of state agencies, yet they still suffer. Children like Timmy James are products of our culture. They act out what they feel, see, and learn from their family and larger society.

You are probably a parent who has taken your role very seriously, learning all you can about healthy child development. But sometimes life gets in the way and hinders you from being the kind of parent you dream of being. Many of the plans you have to be the perfect parent and to raise the perfect child have gotten lost in the busyness of daily life.

Let's take a closer look at Timmy's parents, who are not caught up in smoking marijuana or hitting their children when they are disagreeable. Let's look at a typical family, one of those all-American types you hear about—two parents and three children who live at the end of a cul-de-sac in a lively neighborhood.

Jim and Sharon James are both 36 and have been married 12 years. They had children right away, in spite of the fact that Jim's work was unsteady at first. After working as a custodian for Safeway and then as an auto mechanic at a friend's garage, he settled into his current profession as a long-haul truck driver. Jim enjoys his driving job, though he grumbles about the poor wages, the tighter restrictions on his driving schedule, and the number of hours he spends away from home. Jim also enjoys being a father, but he feels frustrated with the problems his kids develop and his inability to be available to help his wife solve them.

Sharon likes her job and enjoys the fast pace of the office. She too resents the hours her job demands, but she is grateful for a well-paying job because she knows her husband may have some lean weeks. She appreciates the opportunity to work for the extras in the family. She knows she is gone a lot during the week, but she tries to make up for her absence by giving the children more attention on the weekends.

Jim and Sharon agreed to have children, though Sharon was the one who wanted the larger family. She likes the feeling of having a house full of rambunctious children. She is concerned about Timmy, however, and annoyed by the increasing number of phone calls she receives from the school.

Both Jim and Sharon resent the way Timmy's problems intrude into their already hectic lives and take them away from their interactions with their other children. Timmy's siblings resent him. They watch angrily as Timmy absorbs the energy of the family. He has become increasingly aggressive with them as well, and the other children have begun avoiding him and calling him Trouble. The sibling rivalry is heating up, and Sharon and Jim feel incapable of managing the conflict.

In spite of their hectic schedules, the Jameses find time to be involved with church. They are strong Christians and attend a local nondenominational church every week, and all three children attend Sunday school classes. The family feels more warmth and cohesion on the Sundays when Jim is home from the road and they are able to spend time together as a family. Timmy particularly enjoys these times. He pushes for the family to sit down together for meals and play board games in the evenings. These are often enjoyable times for the family.

The Family as a System

Though Timmy's siblings call him Trouble and he is the focus of much critical energy by the family, he is not the only problem.

Whatever happens in the family is everyone's problem. This is the perspective of the family therapist who might consider Timmy's plight. We might be tempted to focus on Timmy alone, but we are probably better off thinking about what might be going on within the family. We want to take a larger point of view when thinking about Timmy, his self-image, and the internal struggles that cause him to act out. In fact, we must see acting out—behaviorally expressing inner issues—from a larger point of view.

Virginia Satir, the renowned family therapist and author of *Peoplemaking,* was one of the first to educate us that children are created by families. Of course, parents are instrumental in the initial making of children, but the unique makeup of families takes over from there.

Satir further indicates that families have their own unique identities. The family is a dynamic organism that is more than the sum of its parts. An organic interdependency exists among members of any social system, similar to the relationship between parts of our physical bodies. Interestingly, the apostle Paul used the same analogy when describing the dynamic organism of the church: "Just as each one of us has one body with many members, and these members do not all have the same function, so in Christ we who are many form one body, and each member belongs to all the others" (Romans 12:4-5).

What a wonderful description of the human body, the body of Christ, and yes, the human family. We are connected. We live and breathe together, impacting one another for good and sometimes for ill.

The whole family shapes the values, attitudes, and behaviors of each member. Conscious and unconscious family rules and expectations, patterns of power, and taboos affect everyone in the family.

Nathan Ackerman, renowned family therapist and author of *The Psychodynamics of Family Life,* suggests the family has such an impact on individuals that change is nearly impossible unless the entire family makes a significant shift. The family must change in positive directions to support the individuals' growth. In fact, the goal of family therapy is to change the underlying rules and patterns so that all members will be free to grow, and none will be used as a scapegoat to bear the hidden family pain.

Ackerman says the term *organism* points to the family's living process, which he describes as "a period of germination, a birth, a growth and development, a capacity to adapt to change and crisis, a slow decline, and finally, dissolution of the old family into the new."

I am the product of a large and relatively healthy family. My father, however, is the adult child of an alcoholic, and my mother's parents suffered an early and embarrassing divorce. She was raised by her mother and stepfather and had two younger half-siblings. With this heritage, we were raised with fairly rigid family rules—our family had a right way to do things, a strict code of family behavior.

I appreciated my family upbringing. We were aware early on that my father had been impacted by an alcoholic parent, and thus all liquor was strictly taboo. We honored hard work and respected Christian values and participation in the central life of the church. Most feelings were allowed—except anger. Because we did not allow each other to express anger, I have had a challenge learning how to manage anger in a healthy way.

I have spent years trying to understand my childhood and its impact on my development. I have explored how my parents and their family history shaped my self-image. I have worked arduously to separate my worth from what I produce. Making changes to my personality has been a process of understanding and respecting my past, exploring how I carry my parents' values in my head, and learning how to make appropriate changes. I have worked hard to understand and appreciate the way my family system shaped my identity.

Nature Versus Nurture

As you think about your child and his self-image, consider your family tree. Consider for a moment how he has been impacted by the genetics in your family (nature) and by the family environment, rules, and structure (nurture).

Let's consider your child's innate disposition. From early on, my oldest son clearly had the innate disposition of a thoughtful introvert. From an early age he preferred order to chaos. Unlike me, he preferred to think things out rather than talk them out. He was always a sensitive boy and is now a sensitive young man. However, he was never one to quickly share his feelings. He shared them when he was good and ready. He never seems to have much money. He lives in the here and now. He has been that way since he was two years old—his innate nature.

My youngest son has an entirely different innate disposition. He has always been an extrovert, preferring to talk things out rather than sit and reflect on them. He was more disorderly, prone to having his belongings spread between here and Beijing. He is quick to share his feelings. He wants to be nurtured and seeks love and support. He always has some money, to the chagrin of his older brother.

This issue of nature versus nurture is not news to you. If you have more than one child, you know they come out of the chute very different from one another. Some come out as extroverts, some as introverts. Some are neat and orderly, some live with clutter. Some can't hold onto a cent; others know how to squeeze a dollar out of a dime. Each child is born as a unique individual, and we must understand and appreciate that.

Parents obviously affect their children, but children exert their own influence, changing the family dynamics. As I look back on my sons' early years, I can see how their behavior impacted their mother and me as well as each other. Family members are interrelated. As we explore this issue of self-image, we must keep in mind how the family functions—especially how the family may reinforce self-image problems.

Take a moment to consider these questions:

- How would you describe your family of origin?
- Did your family have enough love to go around? Did you lack love and nurturance?
- Did anyone in your family abuse anyone else physically, sexually, or emotionally?
- If abuse did occur, how did you family deal with it? Did they talk about it openly, or did they hide it?

Now, the most important question: How have these issues impacted your parenting? Take time to think about this. Your childhood doesn't need to dictate the way you raise your children, but it certainly has some effect, and you'll do well to at least consider it.

Rigid and Closed, or Open and Growing

Family systems therapists, who view individual problems from the perspective of the family, provide some tools to understand family functioning and the way it affects a child's self-image. One of the ways to evaluate families is to determine whether the family is open and growing, or closed and rigid.

Open, healthy families have more persons in their family support network and in fact encourage involvement from people outside the immediate family. Open families have several high-quality, extra-familial relationships. Let me illustrate.

When I was growing up, the Hawkins family had many extra-family friendships. We were integrally involved in the Swedish Mission Covenant Church. We were one of those families that were at the church any time the doors were open. The opposite also seemed to be true—people in the church were also at our home. Every Sunday—and I do mean *every* Sunday—we either invited someone to our home for Sunday dinner or we were invited to someone's home. The adults hung out with other adults, and the kids played with other children.

In addition to our involvement with the church, my family had an open-door policy in our neighborhood. My mother was often at our neighbors', the Silsbees', or Mrs. Silsbee was at our home. Our family and neighborhood motto was "Come on in. The coffee's always on."

Of course, with this kind of family openness, we kept no secrets from our friends. They knew how the Hawkins family lived, and we knew how our neighbors and friends lived.

A closed family, in contrast, keeps to themselves. "The way we live is nobody's business," closed parents might tell their children. "Our secrets are nobody's business." They have few friends, and their boundaries are rigidly defined by tall, sturdy fences—figuratively and sometimes even literally. Closed, rigid families are extremely vulnerable to crises. They resist change and try desperately to maintain the status quo with inflexible rules and by coercion. In contrast, open families tend to cope more constructively with crises and change. They are more open to revising and negotiation.

Open, growth-oriented families are obviously much more suitable for raising children with a healthy self-image.

- They accept feelings.
- They honor disagreements.
- They share opinions openly.
- They communicate openly.
- Their rules are flexible.
- They appreciate family differences.

Contrast the closed, rigid family:

- They do not accept many feelings.

- They do not tolerate disagreements.
- They discourage opinions.
- They stifle communication.
- Their rules are inflexible.
- They discourage family differences.

Take a moment to review the above list. How did your family of origin fare? How is your current family? Is your family open and growth oriented, or is it closed and rigid? What can you do to move in a positive direction?

Here are some practical steps to become a more growth oriented and open family.

Practice communicating your needs and feelings openly. Encourage family members to share their feelings, needs, and desires openly. Even if the desires cannot be fulfilled, express hopes and dreams openly.

Encourage the healthy expression of conflict. Discourage attacks on any member of the family. Express negative feelings in healthy ways—never by attacking anyone's character.

Practice resolving conflicts together. Join as a family to solve problems. Encourage creative expression and problem solving. All family members should share their thoughts and feelings on a matter, as well as ways they might solve a current problem.

Balance the need for togetherness with the need for autonomy. Encourage more autonomy within the family. Allow each person to be an individual rather than simply a member of the family.

Develop more supportive relationships with other people, families, and institutions. Find ways to invite families into your home. Get more involved in your church. See how other families live, share, and solve problems.

Finally, experiment with new behaviors and ways of relating that are more responsive to the real needs of the family. Encourage every member to be open about hurts, fears, and hopes for the family. Look for new, creative ways of being individuals in your family.

Families are God-given places for us to develop. You may be tempted to compare your family to the one down the street, but that is not likely to be helpful. Rather, assess your family's situation according to the set of standards and techniques mentioned in this chapter. Find a few areas where you can grow as a family and set about making positive changes. Select one or two small areas to focus on for change—celebrate the results!

4

The Psychological Needs
of a Child

A child's self-image does not develop in a vacuum. Just as an acorn needs the right soil and sunshine to grow into a mighty oak, children need the right conditions to grow into healthy adults with strong, solid self-concepts. To explore ways to develop a child's self-image, we need to understand the optimal conditions under which children grow.

We also need to understand that building a child's self-image is not optional. This is not some metaphysical concept concocted to sell books. A healthy self-image, that positive, core attitude about who you are as a person, is critical to your well-being throughout life.

Do you recall when your child was born? The first moments of my sons' lives were incredible and absolutely awe inspiring, if not terrrifying. I cried at their births, feeling a profound connection with God as I witnessed these two human beings enter the world.

I distinctly recall looking at them and asking God, *How is this possible? How can a fully formed human being come into this world? Those tiny toes, the tender pink skin, the rheumy eyes trying so hard to focus. This is not possible, God, apart from Your miraculous work. And You're inviting me into cocreation with You?*

Of course, life in general and our children's lives in particular aren't possible apart from God. How anyone can watch a birth and be an atheist is beyond my understanding. As we consider the psychological needs of children, which include a healthy self-image, we must again remind ourselves of our origin.

> I praise you because I am fearfully and wonderfully
>   made;
>   your works are wonderful,
>   I know that full well.
> My frame was not hidden from you
>   when I was made in the secret place.
> When I was woven together in the depths of the
>   earth,
>   your eyes saw my unformed body (Psalm 139:14-
>   16).

Once we have the bundle of joy—or screaming little human—in our arms, what do we do with her? Raise her, of course. Yes, but things are a little more complex than that. While we know we must take our child to the doctor if she spikes a fever, we aren't as clear about what to do about her emotional well-being. In fact, you may not have given a lot of thought to the notion that you must offer your child certain qualities and avoid certain actions to build her self-image—which is one of her primary needs for healthy adulthood.

Let's consider some of a child's basic psychological needs and see how they help create a healthy self-image.

Security and stability. Most authorities would agree that children need security to thrive. You are probably aware that you do better when your world is stable and secure. The same is even truer for a child.

I have been building a new home for the past 18 months. During that time I have been buying new items for the house, many of which I have had to place in storage. As the months have passed and the building has slowly progressed, more of my energy has been attached to the new house. Unfortunately, this has also added a lot of stress to my life. No longer stable in my primary home, I feel displaced at times. I am on the road back and forth between my old home and my new home. My anchors, so to speak, have been pulled. I feel adrift.

Perhaps you have experienced a transition. It can easily give you an unsettled feeling. As you consider this feeling, you will empathize with children's needs for stability and security. They need to know they will be staying in one place with one set of caregivers (parents), and they need to know they can expect some consistency in the future. Children require a predictably stable life.

Fear can be a real issue for children. They are often little sponges that absorb their parents' emotions. When divorce happens, or the loss or change of a job forces a move, children feel their world shake. When conflict is in the home, children develop a low-level anxiety as they absorb the tension. They know when life is unstable and their world is threatened. They know that if something drastic happens to Mom and Dad, their whole world will change dramatically. When they are using all their energies just to absorb the fear, they don't have enough left over to grow and explore their world. Even a little fear can devastate a child, stunting his emotional growth, and parents must do everything they can to manage it properly.

Confidence. When children feel secure and enjoy the stability of loving parents, they are able to grow emotionally. Feeling at peace, they are able to explore their worlds, developing confidence to handle different circumstances. Ideally, parents will encourage their children to face new challenges and find solutions to their problems. This experience creates self-confidence and is the foundation for a healthy self-image.

Consider the young child who comes home from school and

whimpers about being picked on by another child, perhaps her best friend. You may be tempted to either ignore her complaints or offer a quick remedy, but a more helpful alternative would be to encourage her to find a solution to the problem. Listening to her concerns and expressing confidence in her ability to find solutions, you will empower her to develop problem-solving skills and self-confidence.

Consider the teenager who comes home brimming with pride for having won an academic contest. You have the opportunity to comment and show pride not only in his accomplishment but also in his hard work, which led to the achievement.

Love. Who could survive a day without the knowledge that she is loved? This is such a basic necessity. We all need to know that we are special and loved by someone. But how is love expressed? We may say we love our children, or our mates, but if we don't express our love appropriately, it will not have the desired effect. Consider these expressions of love for your child:

- Verbally express caring and affection.
- Offer physical contact with him.
- Pay attention to the details of his life.
- Listen to his stories.
- Allocate time to attend his school and sporting events.
- Empathize with him during times of stress.

Feeling unconditional love is critical for your child. Offering praise and attention when she has done extremely well on an exam is just as important as offering love and support when she simply needs a tender hug after a tough day at school.

Consider the biblical story of the prodigal son. The story is poignant and especially meaningful as it illustrates the love our heavenly Father has for us. Let's read how Luke tells the story.

There was a man who had two sons. The younger one said to his father, "Father, give me my share of the estate." So he divided his property between them.

Not long after that, the younger son got together all he had, set off for a distant country and there squandered his wealth in wild living. After he had spent everything, there was a severe famine in that whole country, and he began to be in need. So he went and hired himself out to a citizen of that country, who sent him to his fields to feed pigs. He longed to fill his stomach with the pods that the pigs were eating, but no one gave him anything.

When he came to his senses, he said, "How many of my father's hired men have food to spare, and here I am starving to death! I will set out and go back to my father and say to him: Father, I have sinned against heaven and against you. I am no longer worthy to be called your son; make me like one of your hired men." So he got up and went to his father.

But while he was still a long way off, his father saw him and was filled with compassion for him; he ran to his son, threw his arms around him and kissed him. The son said to him, "Father, I have sinned against heaven and against you. I am no longer worthy to be called your son." But the father said to his servants, "Quick! Bring the best robe and put it on him. Put a ring on his finger and sandals on his feet. Bring the fattened calf and kill it. Let's have a feast and celebrate. For this son of mine was dead and is alive again; he was lost and is found." So they began to celebrate.

I have been moved whenever I have read this story, whether for the first or one hundred and forty-first time. The father typifies God, the younger son corresponds to the repentant sinner, and the older son represents the scribes and Pharisees, or those of us who lean toward being legalistic.

The younger son is a prodigal son, one who is recklessly extravagant and who spends his money wastefully. I can relate. As a teenager, I wanted to get away from my parents' authority as soon as possible. Much like this prodigal, I wanted to make my own way in the world. And much like this young, foolish son, I squandered their love, living a self-centered life.

This son wanted his portion of the estate immediately, refusing to wait for his father to die. He left a good life for one of sinful pleasures, but before long he was destitute, and the only job he could get was feeding pigs. He must not have taken long in these deplorable conditions to realize that being back home, even feeding pigs there, would be better than enduring the life he was living under his own authority.

We then see a turn in the son's character. Humbled, he realized that he was no longer worthy of being called a son, and he determined to return home as a servant. Then we read some of my favorite words in all Scripture, a verse that is certainly suitable to our discussion of a parent's love for his child.

> But while he was still a long way off, his father saw him and was filled with compassion for him; he ran to his son...

These words stick to my ribs. They touch my heart and soul, for I have experienced this unconditional love as an earthly son with my father and also as a son with my heavenly Father. When I was a long way off, stuck in my rebellion and wayward living, my earthly and heavenly fathers ran to me and reached out with their loving arms to embrace me. What could be sweeter than to feel compassion when you are bruised and battered, muddied by life? My fathers could have rejected me; they could have given me what I deserved—to be chastised, scolded, and shamed. But instead I received love.

Even if you have not experienced the unconditional love of an earthly father, I encourage you to picture Father God running to sweep you into His welcoming arms. You may, like the prodigal son, be ragged and muddy, but God is ready to embrace you. He is ready to embrace your children too, regardless of how they have behaved.

Communication. Another basic need children have is to communicate with others and to be noticed. One of the surest ways children experience love is through daily communication. Children need to spend time every day communicating with their parents and siblings. That's when they learn about themselves and others. As they share their emotions, they learn that recognizing and expressing their feelings is normal and healthy. Emotions, incidentally, are an integral part of self-image. Learning how to manage emotions is a huge part of growing up.

Communication not only feels good, it is a primary ingredient of meaningful relationships. As children learn to communicate and listen, they develop primary building blocks of healthy relationships. Healthy relating is an integral piece of our core personality and self-image.

We want children to be able to look in the mirror and say, "I can communicate effectively. I can tell my parents and friends what I think, feel, and want. I have confidence in my ability to talk about myself and listen to others as they share about themselves. I can set my needs aside at times to listen to others."

Attention. Certainly a variation on the theme of communication is the idea of giving attention to a child. Consider how a child feels when our actions say, "You are important enough to me that I will give you my undivided attention. I want to know what you think, how you are feeling, and what you need."

I remember being a ten-year-old boy playing summer-league baseball at Carl Cozier Elementary School. I enjoyed playing baseball, and I especially liked the fact that my parents took time to come and watch me play. I'm sure I gave them mixed messages about seeing them there, but their participation in this part of my life was important to me deep down. I was important enough for them to come and watch a bunch of gangly, uncoordinated kids play something mimicking the sport of baseball. For 25 years I have tried to show the same respect and enthusiasm for my two sons.

Showing our children attention is not optional. We cannot show our love without showing interest in them and what they enjoy. We cannot say we love our children and yet not show them consideration, especially at those critical moments in their lives when they need someone present.

Bonding. Much has been written about the parent-child bond, that unique interplay between the child and caregiver and its foundational role in all future relationships. It is imperative for a healthy self-image and for emotional well-being. Secure bonding creates feelings of safety and predictability, and it forms the basis for positive mental health.

This is powerful stuff. Consider that the strength and health of your relationship with your child will be the model and premise for all his future relationships. Wow! If your relationship is fragile and chaotic, chances are his future relationships may be fragile and chaotic as well.

I performed a psychological evaluation recently on a young woman whose children were taken away because she failed to provide a safe and stable environment for them. Serious questions arose about her availability and attachment to her children. Her children showed symptoms of not being attached to their mother, and this alarmed social workers. The mother was devastated that her children had been taken away. She felt like an utter failure as a mother. She felt shocked and ill-equipped to remedy the situation, and she shared the following story.

"My parents divorced when I was young. I moved around between my mom, my dad, and my aunt and uncle. I think I went to ten different schools in my life. As soon as I started getting closer to my mom, I was moved again. As soon as I got attached to my aunt and uncle, I was moved again. I don't know how to be stable for my kids. I don't know how anyone can expect me to be stable when no one has been stable for me my whole life."

This woman raises a good point, and we must try to understand her plight. How can we expect her to bond with her children when she did not enjoy that kind of bond or stability with her parents? Yet she is responsible to recognize and end the cycle. Her children need a stable home where they can develop a healthy attachment so that they can have secure and strong relationships in the future.

We know a lot about the parent-child bond. People may take it for granted, but many children have not enjoyed a strong parent-child relationship. The result is devastating. We dare not overlook the powerful impact a parent can have by making eye contact, touching, holding, talking, and singing to a child. We cannot say enough about the importance of a mother looking into her infant's eyes and praising the child's unique qualities. These moments provide the foundation for a healthy self-image in the future.

Play. Yes, play provides an important role in a child's healthy emotional and psychological development. Play may look like something kids do to fill up their time, but that is only the tiniest sliver of the truth. Play is actually a very fundamental activity, necessary for children's healthy growth.

> Play is the work of childhood and a vital part of a child's life. Through play, kids develop physically, learn to get along with others, hone specific skills, and explore the world around them. You can track the development of your children through the types of play they undertake.[1]

Play is also vital to physical development. Teaching children how to run, jump, catch a ball, and enjoy themselves encourages development of their fine and gross motor skills. Play can also be a rich time for developing imagination. Playing dress-up, running a make-believe store, and putting on a performance are wonderful opportunities for children to be creative.

Play is also an opportunity to develop problem-solving skills, practice self-control, and learn how to get along with others. What child has not had to struggle with getting along with others while playing a competitive game? These are invaluable moments in a child's development as he is growing in creativity, self-discipline, problem solving, and yes, a healthy self-image. The way a child interacts with his friends and the way his friends respond to him, are powerful influences in the development of self-image.

Discipline. The Scriptures warn us, "He who spares the rod hates his son, but he who loves him is careful to discipline him" (Proverbs 13:24). Discipline is obviously a critical aspect in every child's development.

We hardly needed to read that in the Scriptures, however, to know that the human infant needs boundaries almost from her first breath. A child, left to her own devices, will run a family—and possibly ruin it. With willpower that puts Napoleon to shame, children left without boundaries and discipline will soon bring parents to their knees.

I am currently counseling two parents, Meg and Sam Benson, regarding their six-year-old son. In short, they said that little Danny was defiant, determined to make their lives miserable. The youngest of four children, Danny would be their last child, and at first his "testiness" was cute. The older siblings all complained about his willfulness and delighted in his creative pursuits of power. However, as the years elapsed and Danny's parents began to see what Danny's future might look like, they decided to set a new course.

Meg and Sam adopted a firmer approach to parenting, and Danny did not like it. In fact, the firmer they became, the more belligerent he acted. His tantrums and outrageous behavior made his parents cry uncle and prompted them to call me for an appointment.

"We don't know what to do. His behavior is getting worse, and the school is telling us we have to get him some help."

"Tell me about his behavior," I said.

"When we tell him to do something, he crosses his arms and laughs at us. I admit, at first we thought this was cute. It was like he was a little sergeant or something. But now he doesn't go to bed when we tell him, he won't eat the things he doesn't like, and he's talking back to his teacher."

"So tell me how you discipline Danny," I suggested.

They looked at one another with raised eyebrows and uplifted hands. Clearly they were lost.

"We don't have a good plan," Meg said sheepishly.

"Nope. Nothing we do seems to work," Sam added.

"Folks, you have raised three other children. How did you discipline them?" I added.

"It seemed easier. For some reason they didn't test us as much as Danny does. And maybe we've been more lax with our last child."

The Bensons wanted me to see Danny right away so I could "fix him," but they soon realized the work would have to come from them. They were with Danny every day, and their style of discipline had created the power vacuum in their parenting. We spent the next several sessions talking about many of the things Dr. James Dobson addresses in his books concerning discipline.

Dobson summarizes many of his beliefs about discipline in his popular book *The Strong-Willed Child*. His exhaustive work on parenting is consistent with parenting principles other specialists promote. He asserts the following concepts, worth every parent's consideration:

- Define the boundaries before they are enforced.

- When defiantly challenged, respond with confident decisiveness.

- Distinguish between willful defiance and childish irresponsibility.

- Reassure and teach after the confrontation is over.

- Avoid impossible demands.

- Let love be your guide![2]

The Bensons needed to set healthy boundaries for their family. They needed this not only for their own sanity but also because children (and adults!) need boundaries. While Danny appeared to enjoy running the show, every child (and adult!) actually desires to have healthy boundaries. Everyone needs to know the limits and function within them. Boundaries create safety!

Dobson's list is not exhaustive, but these emotional and psychological needs for discipline are universal in children. By meeting these needs, you will provide another building block for your child's healthy self-image.

5

Children and Families
Who Struggle

In a perfect world, every child would have a fair chance to develop a strong, healthy self-image, to dream lofty dreams, and to set his sights for the stars. Sadly, the world does not offer a level playing field. Some kids will have greater chances than others.

"Be all you can be." "What your mind can conceive, you can believe and achieve." "Just do it."

These affirmations are all good. We can accomplish great things. Some people are like Helen Keller, able to overcome incredible obstacles to achieve astonishing things.

But many fall by the wayside, ending up in various forms of trouble. Consider these alarming statistics, published by the National Association of Self-Esteem:

- One-fifth of all eighth graders in the United States are considered to be at high risk of school failure.
- Approximately 30 percent of our youth drop out and fail to complete high school.
- Homicide is now the nation's third leading cause of death

for elementary and middle-school children. There were 2,555 juvenile homicides in 1990.

- It is estimated that 135,000 guns are brought into schools every day. Violence in schools is now the primary concern of educators nationwide, and 82 percent report a significant increase in violence over the past five years.[1]

These statistics are alarming and should cause us to ask serious questions. Why is this happening? Are these statistics reflections of our kids' self-image? A review of the research indicates that an unhealthy self-image is strongly associated with problems like these:

- poor school performance
- crime and violence
- teenage pregnancy
- alcohol and drug abuse
- school dropouts
- suicide
- eating disorders[2]

Do you see the correlation between the alarming statistics and self-image? This list highlights a significant problem. A healthy self-image is not optional—it is mandatory if our children are to succeed in life.

Symptoms of Unhealthy Self-Image

Let's revisit Timmy James and consider how he exhibits symptoms of a child struggling with a poor self-image.

Timmy is on a path that could easily lead to delinquency, poor academic achievement, drug and alcohol abuse, a tendency toward anger and violence, mental health problems, and a poor self-image. Why do I make such a harrowing prognosis? Am I making a mountain out of a molehill? No. Consider Timmy's symptoms.

- He has trouble making healthy friendships.
- He is not cooperative with authority.
- He shows tendencies of not controlling his behavior.
- He does not follow age-appropriate rules.
- He complains that others dislike him.
- He feels that he cannot excel at new tasks.

We dare not label Timmy as a failure, but he clearly displays symptoms of a poor self-image. Without immediate intervention, he is likely to get into further trouble in years ahead. Labels such as *troublemaker, low achiever,* or *delinquent* can be very difficult to overcome.

Timmy and his family need intervention. He is being evaluated for symptoms associated with attention deficit hyperactivity by a child psychiatrist who specializes in such disorders. In counseling we are helping Timmy learn social skills that will help him make healthy friendships. We are creating opportunities for him to excel, so he will learn that he really is able to master new tasks. We are seeking creative outlets—ways he can use his energies to express himself creatively, such as building models, pursuing musical interests, and even exploring artistic endeavors. He is participating in structured athletics to gain physical skills.

Even with all of these opportunities, however, Timmy needs a functional family, with parents who are willing to create an environment where he can thrive. I am helping the family to recognize that the problem is larger than Timmy; the entire family must create feelings of cohesiveness and support.

Does Your Child Have a Low Self-Image?

As you read this book, you undoubtedly wonder about your child and whether he has a healthy self-image. You have learned about the symptoms of a child with a poor self-image. Now we move forward, exploring remedies for these problems. Before doing so, however, let's review some red flags of children with self-image issues.

- Does your child constantly run himself down by making derogatory comments about himself?
- Does your child doubt her abilities, and is she afraid to develop new ones?
- Is your child submissive, preferring to defer decision making and responsibilities to others?
- Is your child indecisive?
- Does your child have difficulty managing frustration?
- Does your child become anxious in new situations?
- Does your child withdraw from and feel rejected by peers?
- Does your child appear to be sad or unhappy much of the time?

If you answered yes to any of these questions, you have reason for concern—but solutions are available. Any yes answer points you in the direction of issues that need attention.

Families in Trouble

All infants are born without a sense of self. Their self-image develops mostly by means of the mirroring that takes place within the family. Parents have a huge responsibility to create an environment where children can develop a positive self-image. Too often this does not happen, and children develop a poor self-image. Children in trouble with their self-image often grow up in families with multiple problems. Let's briefly look at several.

Conditional, performance-based love and acceptance. Tragically, many families dole out love and acceptance as if they were M&M's given for good performance. Children learn to feel good about themselves if they do exactly what their parents expect. Love is earned, not freely given. Kids learn to tune in to parental expectations, and the motivated ones strive to please. At times they give up trying, knowing they will never fully meet their parents' expectations.

This malady plagues many adults today, including me. I grew up in a loving home, but I gained greater acceptance by performing well, and as I enjoyed the attention and praise for my performance, I learned to work even harder. Sadly, I passed on some of these traits to my sons. Inadvertently I praised them for their achievements more than for their character traits. We have spent much time over the past few years clarifying that they are valuable simply because of who they are.

Repressed emotions. This is a tricky one, and again I am guilty. How can we allow our children to affirm and embrace every feeling when those very same feelings make us feel uncomfortable? This, I'm afraid, is one of those difficult aspects of parenting.

Picture this scenario: Your child comes home from school and complains that his best friend rejected him. That's an easy one, you say. You immediately launch into all the reasons why your child should not feel rejected, thinking you are building his self-confidence. (Wrong. Your child needs understanding and empathy.)

How about this one? Your child is angry because she feels picked on by her stepparent, your spouse. You quickly tell her she should feel thankful her stepparent has agreed to be a part of this family. You offer a litany of benefits that come from the stepparent's involvement in the family. (Nope. Your daughter needs space to have her feelings and safety to explore why she might be feeling the way she does.)

Or, your son tells you he is frightened about an upcoming performance at school. You tell him he has nothing to be frightened about. (Again, this does not accept your child's feelings and his right to have them.)

These situations occur frequently in families. Children have experiences every day with accompanying feelings. Their lives are often emotional roller coasters, but parents view situations differently and often impatiently dismiss their children's feelings. Without intending to, they create an environment where children learn to either suppress feelings or, even worse, to disengage from them. Children's self-image is damaged in the process.

Unresolved problems. Dysfunctional families seem to be anxious about anxiety. Problems are problematic. Rather than openly respecting problems, discussing them, and utilizing their creative strength to solve them, these families panic. One or both of the parents push the panic button—"Oh no, Houston. We have a horrible problem. Catastrophe." All the while, children learn either not to share their problems or to fear them.

Secrets. Yes, many families are secretive. Perhaps Daddy has a drinking problem, and the kids learn to keep quiet about it. Maybe sexual abuse has occurred somewhere in the family tree—often a taboo topic. For a variety of reasons, children learn not to talk about family functioning outside of the family. "What happens in our home is nobody else's business." Sadly, this secretive and shameful attitude spills over into the child's self-image. "Something must be wrong with me too because I'm part of it." So the family maintains the public image at all costs.

Lack of open and honest communication. Unhealthy families communicate in indirect and unconstructive ways. Parents give unclear, inconsistent, contradictory, or confusing messages to their children. They teach their children, directly or indirectly, not to share what they feel, not to think what they think, not to recognize and be able to interpret verbal and nonverbal cues. This, of course, is extremely disabling to children, who are trying to make sense of their world.

John Bradshaw, in his popular book *Bradshaw On: The Family,* says, "Clear and consistent communication are keys to establishing separateness and intimacy—clear communication demands awareness of self and the other, as well as mutual respect for each other's dignity."[3]

Consider what happens when a child has a thought but fears sharing it, or when a child has a feeling but has not been taught how to express it. Personal hurt and pain intensify under the pressure of isolation. These are very troubling and debilitating experiences for the child.

Few displays of affection. Many families have trouble openly expressing warmth and affection. In these cold families, children feel as if they have a hole in their soul. Something has happened in the parents' background that hinders them from being openly loving.

Just last evening I was with my great-niece Emma. I enjoyed watching this rambunctious two-year-old climb up and down from our laps, soaking up hugs and natural affection. Secure in our love, she meandered from aunt to uncle, from activity to activity, knowing she could always find open and welcome arms. I couldn't help thinking that this will help her grow into a secure and confident adult with a strong and healthy self-image.

Addiction. Of course, addictions cause an avalanche of other problems. When a parent or any other family member struggles with addictions, the entire family experiences problems with communication, repression of feelings, denial of problems, and avoidance of responsibility.

The addict's self-image cannot help but be hurt by his addiction, and this causes problems for the whole family. This parent will be incapable of providing the secure, stable, and loving world a child needs to develop. The parent transfers his negative self-image to the child.

A Closer Look

As I counseled the James family, I quickly discovered significant problems. The problems were not as simple as getting Timmy to pay attention in school or choose better friends. The problems were more severe and are typical of families with self-image problems:

- a sense of insecurity
- an inability to play and have fun
- an inability to tolerate stress
- an inability to handle conflict and tolerate disagreements
- an inability to effectively solve problems
- a problem with sharing emotions and intimacy
- an inability to communicate openly and effectively
- an inability to trust and respect one another
- an inability to set healthy boundaries

As I became familiar with the James family, I realized they had much work to do. However, I shared with them an important phrase that may be helpful to you as well: *Aim for progress, not perfection.* Each of us is a work in progress.

As I've worked with Timmy's parents, they have slowly developed an understanding of issues they learned as children and have now passed along to their children. We joined forces and set to work on healing many of the issues that were hurting both them and their children. We identified the specific behaviors that were particularly hurtful to Timmy and the rest of their children. We focused on the healing strategies that we will highlight in the next chapter.

6

Building Your Child's Self-Image

Recognizing how we hamper a child's growing self-image is one thing; developing a plan to strengthen a child's self-image is quite another. We may catch ourselves doing something destructive, yet changing these destructive patterns is often far more difficult than we first expected. Diagnosing the problem is often easier than following through with the remedy.

I remember the years of my sons' adolescence, thankfully some time ago now. During those years I was often frustrated and angry with them for leaving their bikes in the driveway, for pushing the limits on their curfews, for leaving their dirty underwear all over the bedroom floor, for nearly anything. I recognized my inflated need for them to follow the rules, yet changing this damaging pattern was an arduous task.

Why should I have to be the one to change? I groused to myself.

Because, my more mature self would answer, *you need to change. What are you doing? Being so angry with them only pushes them away. It does nothing to correct their behavior or bring them closer to you.*

Ah, but that is more mature than I want to be. I want them to change, I persisted.

Yes, my more mature self said, *that would make things simple, wouldn't it? But they are kids. They are going to make poor choices. They need opportunities to make more effective choices.*

And so the internal argument continued until I usually reluctantly surrendered, deciding in spite of their choices I was going to do my best to have reasonable responses to their actions. I was going to *act*, not *react*. I was going to thoughtfully choose how to be the best father I could be. Usually.

You too can choose how you will act with your children. You can make choices that will build strong, healthy self-images in your children, launching them effectively into adulthood. But where to begin?

Roots of Happiness and Self-Image

Dr. Edward Hallowell, author of *The Childhood Roots of Adult Happiness,* lists five critical tools every child needs to grow into a strong and healthy adult. These five strategies are wonderful ways to enhance your child's self-image.

Connection. Much like bonding, discussed earlier in this book, connection helps children feel safe and secure in relationship to their parents and others. Children must know, regardless of their behavior, they will be loved and attached to their family.

> Connection—in the form of unconditional love from an adult, usually one or both parents—is the single most important childhood root of adult happiness…By growing up with a strong feeling of connectedness, a child develops a sense of what Erik Erikson called *basic trust* early on. The child also develops a feeling of security and safety, which in turn, instills courage and the desire to take risks in the world—whether at six months of age or sixty years.[1]

Play. I have mentioned the importance of play. Play is the work of childhood. As much as some of us parents want to motivate our children to do something more productive, we must remember that play is productive and is a critical activity of childhood.

Play builds imagination. Play teaches children to interact effectively with other children. Solitary play teaches children to explore the reaches of their mind, perhaps through constructing imaginary buildings out of Legos or scripting the next bestselling novel in a diary.

Hallowell says, "Play generates joy. Play becomes its own reward." When we watch a child at play, we see the glow of happiness. We watch her become comfortable in her own skin. We see her self-image blossom and grow.

Practice. Hallowell says a child who plays will soon learn the power of practice. Perhaps a boy is riding his bike and falling repeatedly. His parents might not enjoy watching him struggle with the frustration of practice, but they know it is for his own good. They know he must endure the bruises of practice before he finally scoots down the road, thrusting his hand in the air in exultation.

> Learning anything—from riding a bicycle to playing the piano to speaking Spanish—hurts somewhat. This is because you have to go through a phase in which you see how bad you are at it. A phase in which you feel, and are, inept. Often a phase of marginal improvement despite colossal effort. But with encouragement you keep at it. Finally, you see improvement.[2]

At 54 years of age I am embarking on the task of learning to play the piano. I haven't taken lessons for nearly 50 years, and I am afraid. I know that this will be an arduous undertaking, and I have backed out many times.

What if I forget everything the teacher says? I anxiously wonder. *What if my fingers are no longer dexterous enough?*

What if I can't learn at my age?

What if I can learn but I am really bad at it?

Each of these fears revolves through my mind over and over. I brace myself for my first lesson, telling myself that practice makes perfect—or rather that perfect practice makes perfect. I feel like a seven-year-old again. A determined seven-year-old!

Mastery. Thankfully, our efforts don't often end with frustration, anger, and shaking our head screaming, "I'll never get this! It's impossible! I'm soooo stupid!" although we may wonder about those things along the way. No, with practice comes mastery. After a certain amount of practice and self-discipline, a child or adult will experience the wonderful feeling of mastery. At this point the child exclaims, "Wow—I can do it!" with a grin from ear to ear.

> The roots of self-esteem lie not in praise but in mastery. When a child masters something she couldn't do before—from walking to riding a bike to playing the piano to speaking Spanish—her self-esteem naturally rises, whether she receives any praise or not. If you want your child to have a high sense of self-esteem, don't go out of your way to praise her; go out of your way to make sure she experiences mastery in many different ways.[3]

Let's pretend that your son has just heard he has made it onto the junior high basketball team. Consider these two different reactions from his mom.

"Way to go, John. I'm proud of you and glad you made it. You better practice hard—someone is always ready to take your spot."

"Way to go, John. All your hard work and practice really paid off. I've noticed how much time you put into getting that jump shot down. I know you really wanted to be on the team. You have a right to feel mighty proud."

Notice the difference? In the first example, John's mom offers a sparing compliment and statement of pride in his accomplishment but then adds a warning. John will probably feel a hollow sense of encouragement.

In the second example, John's mom doesn't even say she is proud of him. Rather, she notes how hard he worked and affirmed that his accomplishment must feel good to him. John worked hard at something, mastered it, and is reaping the rewards. This acknowledgment and affirmation is likely to stick with the child and reinforce the sequence of practice, frustration, mastery, recognition, and pride.

Recognition. Mastery leads naturally to recognition and affirmation by others. When a toddler walks for the first time, parents provide the cheering section. When a young child rides her bike for the first time, parents are ecstatic.

> Each act of mastery leads to recognition and approval,
> by an ever-widening circle of people, from parents at first
> to extended family to friends to classmates to the whole
> school to your town or business or readership or viewers
> or whatever your largest audience turns out to be.[4]

The issue of expectations, self-image, and recognition has been a challenge for me in raising my two sons. Both are currently in medical school and will soon become physicians. I'm often tempted to proudly announce, "My sons are going to be doctors," forgetting this does not adequately or appropriately define them. Such superficiality is a vain attempt to bolster my ego. I must remind myself what is truly important. "My sons are wonderful, godly young men. They are loving, generous, and thoughtful. They are good friends of mine. I'm proud they have worked hard to go to medical school to become physicians."

Church and Self-Image

My church reinforced these five elements of my positive self-image. I was raised by one set of parents, and they are still together and in love to this day. But I had a much larger family as well—the church. Within the Bellingham Swedish Covenant Church I developed a strong sense of *connection* and acceptance. I had many "parents" who knew me, taught me, and watched over me.

In this extended family I was able to *play*. Not only did I play with the other children in the church, but our family played with their families, going on church retreats, campouts, hikes, and other activities. We had our annual Swedish smorgasbord and enjoyed gathering together.

I had many opportunities to *practice* new skills in this larger, extended family. I practiced singing in small groups, playing my trumpet with a few other struggling brass players, and sharing my testimony before this loving body.

As I practiced singing, playing my trumpet and giving periodic speeches, I gained *mastery*. As I learned new skills, I grew in confidence and continued to take initiative. I became internally motivated to try new tasks, to develop new skills. The church family was a safe place to spread my wings and fly.

Finally, with practice, failure, growth, and mastery came *recognition*. "My, how Dave Hawkins is growing into a fine young man," I heard many times over. Opinions I hadn't cared about before gradually became important to me. Elders in the church recognized my leadership skills and encouraged them. I began to identify with this body, inquiring about its moral behavior and values.

After graduation from high school, while attending Western Washington University, I began having weekly meetings with Pastor Carleton Peterson. Pastor Carleton was part of my larger family. I felt connected to him and sensed that I could try out new ideas with him. He invited me to come in and ask questions—and I had a boatload.

- How does prayer actually work?
- What do you mean by the Trinity? How is that supposed to work?

- Do you mean to tell me Jesus actually died and rose again?
- Do you think Jesus actually did those miracles the Bible talks about?
- What's so bad about a little sin?

In the safety of the pastor's office, I was able to think out loud. Wild thoughts. Disjointed thoughts. But they were my thoughts, and he let me have them. Here, with a man I respected, I was able to figure out exactly what I believed. From connection to recognition—full circle.

Developing Identity

In those many hours in Pastor Carleton's study, while he propped his feet on his desk and stroked his full beard, I figured out what I believed separate from my parents' beliefs. I could have swallowed my parents' theology whole, but that was not my nature, nor is it the nature of any child who desires to develop a separate identity. I had to question, wrestle with, and even reject the beliefs of others to learn what I thought and believed. This is a critical aspect of growth for every child.

Most parents naturally want their children to be well-behaved, to emulate their beliefs and values. However, this is not necessarily what is best for our children. Dorothy Corkille Briggs, author of *Your Child's Self-Esteem,* notes, "Only by practicing separateness can the child capture the feeling of autonomy...A child's capacity to respect others later on is measured by his capacity to respect himself now."[5]

From the two-year-old tyrant demanding her own way, to the awkward eight-year-old unsure of herself, to the fourteen-year-old defying authority, the journey to sturdy and solid self-image is unsteady. But it is a necessary journey. Unless our children are able to forge their own identity, separate from ours, the rest of their lives will be racked with uncertainty. Throughout this journey they must know they are loved for who they are. Though this separateness is challenging at times, it is a critical aspect of their development.

But what if your 15-year-old son says he no longer believes in God and wants to explore other cosmic forces? What if he wants to wear baggy jeans and dye his hair green? Most teenagers, on their way to finding their surest identity, will find some outrageous ways to separate themselves from you. That may include attitudes that are repulsive and that shake your feelings of affection for them—temporarily. Believe me, I've been there.

The wisest counsel I can give the parent of the teenage boy who wants to grow his hair long, pierce every conceivable opening in his body, and stop going to church is this: Give him choices and choose your battles. It's that simple. Decide ahead of time where you will draw the line and find ways to give him choices so he can express his unique identity. If you draw the lines too hard-and-fast, if your teen feels boxed in, he will rebel, and you will lose. If, on the other hand, you allow him to grow his hair long on the condition that he will still attend church, or he may have one piercing but not three, you may still maintain a relationship. The key is to give him room to tell you and the rest of the world that he is unique.

What About Character?

We would do our children a great disservice if we strengthened their self-image without building their character. They need "the right stuff." A strong character is an integral part of a healthy self-image. But what exactly is character? Here's what the authors of *Growing Kids God's Way* say:

> Moral character is the quality of a person's person-
> ality and the moral restraint or encouragement of his
> temperament. When we speak of Christian character, we
> are referring to moral and social excellence.[6]

We don't simply want our kids to have a healthy self-image. We also want our children to have a strong, Christian character—to have a divine standard, not the moral mediocrity we often see in society. These authors suggest that godly character is best exemplified by the presence or absence of three attributes: respect, honor, and honesty. They suggest that these three qualities are critical fibers in the moral fabric of our being. "The parent's job is to take the intangible concepts of *respect, honor* and *honesty* and to make them tangible—to take their abstract meaning and make them concrete."[7] These character qualities are worked out in the following relationships:

- How do children relate to those in authority?
- How positive is their relationship to their parents?
- Do they have respect for their elders?
- Are they able to relate effectively to friends and siblings?
- Do they respect other people's property?
- Do they honor and respect nature?

These six relationships provide a basis for character training. You will do much to develop character if you focus on respect, honor, and honesty in these six pivotal relationships.

Conscience

Respect, honor, and honesty require a developed moral conscience. Children must have an internal sense of right and wrong. They must be able to weigh moral decisions, feel appropriate guilt when they have failed to live up to that standard, and desire to correct mistakes. If children have no awareness that what they are doing is hurtful to themselves and others, they will cause problems for everyone who crosses their path.

But how do children develop a conscience? Positive parenting guides children in ways that are godly and moral. By setting limits and modeling appropriate behavior, parents teach their kids what is right and wrong. Parents are responsible to define moral parameters for children's behavior and provide clear consequences for violating those boundaries.

Children are confused when their parents set standards and then fail to enforce consequences when those standards are broken. These children learn they are above the rules. Children develop morality from parents who are consistent with God-ordained boundaries and empathetically enforce them.

Another Look at Discipline

Children are generally willful. How's that for an understatement? For the first 18 years of their lives, they will usually pursue their own best interests, often disregarding what you consider best for them. The next couple of years are iffy, and finally, by the ripe old age of 23, they may come back to you and give some indication that you were not as brain-dead as they once thought.

Prior to that, they will test the boundaries to see if you are going to enforce them. That's why you need a sound pattern of discipline that works for you and your children. When children test the limits, as they invariably will do, you must be ready with reasonable consequences to let them know that their behavior is intolerable. This predictability is crucial for them to develop a healthy self-image.

I particularly appreciate Jim Fay and Foster Cline's program, Parenting with Love and Logic. Their system of parenting suggests offering your children reasonable choices and boundaries, with clear consequences when they violate the boundaries. Rather than lecturing children for their mistakes, which is so easy to do, parents can bite their lips and simply empathize with children as they enforce rules. To the testy adolescent, a conversation might sound like this:

"I see that you decided to stay out past curfew tonight, keeping your father and me awake past our bedtime. I know how much you were looking forward to going over to your friend's house tomorrow night, but that won't be possible now. We agreed you would be restricted for two nights if you came in late. We'll try again in a few nights."

"But, I *have* to go to Tammy's birthday party. I've been planning it for a month."

"Yes, I know how tough it will be to miss it. She is probably going to be upset with you. I'm so sorry you didn't plan your time better tonight, but you'll probably think further ahead next time."

Consider how these tools might work with a four-year-old caught sneaking cookies from the cookie jar.

"I'm sorry you chose to take those cookies. You've just had your week's worth of dessert. It's going to be tough going without dessert the rest of this week, especially since the family is having cake and ice cream tonight and brownies tomorrow night, and I know how much you like those. I think you might make a better choice next time."

Some of you may be thinking, *Isn't this discipline a bit harsh? Aren't you making too big a deal out of the fact that the family will be having desserts without her the rest of the week?*

These parents created clear boundaries with logical consequences, using empathy without a lecture. The children did not like the consequences, but they understood ahead of time that the consequences would stand. This pattern, performed over and over again, builds a strong, healthy self-image in the child as well as a cohesive family.

"You Can Do It!"

In these examples, the parents made it clear they believed the children could make good choices. Parents need to repeatedly let children know they will have opportunities for "do overs." Tomorrow is another day. Parents must express (1) confidence in the child's ability to make good choices, (2) understanding that the child will not always do so, and (3) assurance that the child will then live with the consequences.

The parents in the examples above made clear, firm statements, giving their children the message that rules were not flexible.

Boundaries work. They work for kids and adults alike. Boundaries are part of God's natural order. They encourage responsibility; when we violate them, negative events occur. When children honor boundaries, they grow, mature, and become responsible adults.

One of parents' major tasks is to teach children they are capable of making choices that will benefit them and others. This sense of capability is the backbone of a healthy self-image. When children understand they are capable of learning new tasks and accomplishing what they set their minds to, a strong and vibrant self-image results.

According to Steven Glenn and Jane Nelson, authors of *Raising Self-Reliant Children in a Self-Indulgent World,* "children are amazingly responsive to outside stimuli. When we are quick to celebrate any little movement in the right direction, we get more results. Celebrating is simply the act of recognizing progress."[8]

Effective parents catch their children doing things right. Catching your child misbehaving is easier, but kids are more responsive to encouragement than to criticism. They love to be caught doing something beneficial.

When helping children develop capabilities, here are a few suggestions. Notice when your children play cooperatively with their siblings and comment about that. Give them repeated opportunities to master playing cooperatively, using time-outs when they choose not to do so. Notice when your children do something helpful around the house. Pay attention to their efforts in school. Catch them being thoughtful of others. Let them know you believe in them and their capabilities. Make an effort to eliminate criticism from your vocabulary.

Following these suggestions will bring surprising results as you and your child learn useful tools for today and many tomorrows.

7

Habits That Harm
Children's Self-Image

Self-image is initially fragile—very fragile. Many people want to believe children are resilient and can bounce back from anything. We comfort ourselves with these notions. After a heartrending divorce or other calamity, we believe if we are careful and sensitive, children will bounce back emotionally.

Children do have some resiliency. However, they are not as buoyant as we want to believe. The struggles of life can wound and scar them.

I met with seven-year-old Michael yesterday. His parents have been divorced for five years. Brought in by his concerned mother, Michael had blond hair that curled uncontrollably, and his blue eyes sparkled with mischief. His broad smile suggested he was in good spirits. I met with him to talk about his parents' divorce and implications for visitation and custody.

In the course of our conversation I asked Michael how he was doing.

"Fine," he said quickly, his eyes darting around the room. After a brief pause he continued, "They're still fighting with each other."

"Your mom and dad?" I asked.

"Yep," he replied sadly.

"Do you get pretty tired of that?" I asked.

He nodded his head, looking down, fighting back the tears forming in his eyes.

"I'll bet you wish they would just get along with each other."

Again he nodded.

Then he looked up and said something that surprised me.

"I hope they'll get back together."

I was taken aback. We had been talking about the years of fighting between his parents, how they had separated and divorced because of their dislike for one another, and still, amid that conflict, he wanted them back together. He had not given up hope that somehow, someway, they would find a path back together.

Sadly, I told Michael that I did not think that would happen. I shared that his parents were quite upset with each other, that it had nothing to do with him, but that there was little chance they would reconcile.

Michael knows this truth but can't truly digest it. He resists knowing it. Part of him knows he must accept the harsh reality that the two people he loves the most do not love one another, and he will never have the family he has created in his mind. He also knows that the day will come when he will have stepparents in his two homes. This is a statistical fact he doesn't like to think about.

Michael's parents are both good people. I've met them both, and I know they want the best for their son. They want to believe their divorce will not adversely affect him. They want to believe their intense anger toward each other will not impact Michael. But it does. He feels it, and in spite of everything, he continues to hope they will get back together and live happily ever after. Everything these parents say about each other will find its way into Michael's heart and potentially damage his self-image.

Resilience or Adaptation

We often say children are resilient. This implies children will meet a crisis, respond favorably to it, and then bounce back to precrisis form. Research, however, now shows that children are not as resilient as we once imagined or hoped. None of us meet a crisis head-on, respond favorably to it, and remain unchanged. Rather, we adapt to the crisis. It changes us.

One of my favorite places to downhill ski is Mt. Bachelor, Oregon. The snow there is abundant, and numerous high-speed quad chairs take skiers to the top of the mountain in minutes. However, Mt. Bachelor has a significant drawback: wind. It is not just your normal, run-of-the-mill wind—it is face-ripping, biting cold that seems to tear your outer layer of skin off. When the wind is blowing, a ride up the mountain makes even the most avid skiers wonder why they are not sitting in the lodge sipping hot chocolate.

Much of the terrain is majestic and grand, but the unprotected crest of the mountain reveals gnarled, disfigured pine trees. The trees in this wind-whipped climate look sickly. They appear beaten down and begging for mercy, but they are alive. They have been bruised and battered, but they have adapted. They certainly are not so resilient that they have returned to their natural condition. Rather, they are twisted and knobby, clinging together for protection. They have adapted.

The same is true with many of our children. They face adversity with courage. Michael is a brave warrior. He stiffens his lip as he talks about his mom and dad saying hostile things about each other. How will this impact him? How will this mighty wind create gnarls and ridges in his personality? How will these incidents impact his self-image?

Children face other "elements" that shape their self-image. Some are easy to correct; others may not be so easy. Remember, however, that children are not as resilient as we want to believe. They are adaptable, and these adaptations form the basis of many personality traits that may need adjustment later in life.

Problematic Parental Patterns

Parenting is something we do day in and day out. For many this becomes second nature—like brushing your teeth or doing the laundry. We often are not aware of the parenting patterns we develop. Thankfully, many of our patterns are positive. Some are not.

A critical aspect of positive parenting is reviewing your patterns—the ones you do without thinking. Like reviewing your budget annually—you do that, don't you?—and getting that yearly doctor's checkup, looking at your parenting patterns can help you avoid problems. Let's list some problematic parenting patterns that you may need to eliminate.

Criticism

Few parents set out to hurt or humiliate their children. We love our children and do not want to damage their self-image. However, criticism—even constructive criticism, if such a thing exists—can do just that.

Most parents seem to believe that they must correct and criticize their child's behavior to improve it. We notice our children doing something wrong, and like a fireman seeing smoke, we believe we must immediately extinguish the "fire," regardless of the damage to the children. Put out the fire, worry about water damage later.

Parents are often perfectionists. On a quest to create the perfect child, we want the best, and anything less than that causes us to jump into action. We pay attention to some details that perhaps we should ignore.

Years ago I became entrenched in a destructive pattern. When I came home from work, I immediately noticed my sons' bikes lying on the driveway. I immediately shifted into action. Scanning the area with radarlike precision, I noticed a few of my tools lying in the grass. By now I was fuming. I marched into the house and found both sons plopped in front of the television, controls in hand, playing their favorite video game. I was on a mission to seek and destroy. I wanted to seize control of the situation and enforce a regimented behavior code, or so I thought.

Well, you can imagine this scene. Two sons lazing on the couch having fun, suddenly met by an angry father who found fault in everything they were doing. I thought everything they had done was wrong, and I was determined to criticize and make corrections. You can imagine their reaction.

"What's the matter with you?" one son protested.

The other flew to his defense.

"Yeah, we didn't do anything wrong. We're just playing some games before doing our homework."

Their explanations did little to assuage my anger, so they became more defensive and angry, and an argument was well on the way. Nothing productive ever came out of these incidents.

To criticize is to judge, evaluate, blame, censure, and condemn. I did all those things, naively thinking that somehow all of those behaviors would help shape my sons into godly people with strong, healthy self-concepts. Was I ever wrong!

Parents rarely change children's behavior by condemning or judging their actions. In fact, criticism often reinforces the very behavior parents are trying to change. Children take criticism very personally. It often makes them feel as if they are bad people, and they begin to internalize the negative comments. If criticized for being lazy, they are more likely to become or feel lazy. If criticized for being insensitive, they are more likely to behave insensitively. They rationalize that if the parent thinks they are bad, it must be so.

Many children respond to criticism by becoming defensive and retaliating with hostility and defiance. This was my sons' common reaction. They often became defiant, angry, and quite sullen after I criticized them for their behavior. You'd think I would have gotten the message that my reaction was not helpful in changing their behavior, nor was it building their character in any way.

Young children are particularly susceptible to criticism. Seeing themselves through their parents' eyes, they tend to accept their parents' criticism as true and react by giving up on a task rather than risking failure. They are especially hungry to receive recognition and to be highly regarded, and criticism lets the air out of their balloon. You can almost hear the whoosh when speaking negatively about your child.

Does criticism spur positive change? Does it bring about the desired growth in a child? No. Criticism only reinforces insecure feelings the child already has and erodes his or her fragile self-confidence.

Rejection

In today's quick-paced world, filled with myriad distractions, many children are clamoring for their parents' attention. The following scenario happens in many households on a daily basis.

> "Daddy, look at what I painted today in school."
> "Don't interrupt me right now. I'm busy."

Or how about this one?

> "Mom, I need your help with this math. I don't get it."
> "How do you expect me to help you? I was hardly able to do my own math when I was in school."

Both innocent situations. Both well-meaning parents. Every parent has been in this kind of situation more than once. But consider for a moment the impact on the child. What might a child feel if she heard those words from her parent? Consider a child's internal reacton.

> "Dad, I am so excited about what I painted today in school. I want to show it off to you so you can be as proud of me as I am of myself. Pushing me away makes me feel unimportant to you. It makes me think less of myself, as if I am not as important as what you are doing. I won't interrupt you again."

> "Mom, I think you're the smartest person in the world. I am asking for your help because I'm struggling, and I hoped you would help me. Your harsh words make me feel like I've been bad. I won't ask for your help again."

We might think these encounters are benign, having no particular effect on the child. Unfortunately, if these situations happen again and again in various forms, they can stifle a child's enthusiasm. She could begin to doubt her own abilities and feel insecure.

Consider how children feel when someone rejects them. Rejection—being pushed away physically or emotionally—has a particularly harmful impact on a child's sense of belonging. It can be terribly confusing. Children need to know they are important, valued and even prized. When they feel accepted and loved by the people who are important to them, they feel comfortable, safe, secure, and open to communication. If children feel respected and secure within their family, they will easily move outside the family, explore their world, and form healthy attachments.

Rejection is difficult for children to understand. If a parent gets impatient or angry, or struggles with volatile moods, loving one minute and rejecting the next, the child cannot make sense of it. *What am I doing that is making my parents push me away? What is so terribly wrong with me?* Children (and many adults) have little ability to understand these actions and reactions, and they don't realize that they did nothing to cause the rejection.

The noted author Pia Melody suggests children are born with two basic questions: Who am I? and How do I do it? John Bradshaw, in his book *Bradshaw On: The Family,* says, "In order to grow, children need their parents' attention, time, affirmation of their feelings, direction and good modeling."[1] These primary ingredients for a healthy self-image cannot occur in an atmosphere of rejection.

I am counseling with a bright and vibrant 17-year-old girl named Danielle. Danielle has a full head of fiery red hair and a strong, athletic build from her training as a soccer and basketball player. With a ready smile, she is always excited to tell me about her academic and athletic accomplishments.

Contrary to her radiant disposition, Danielle has much to be upset about in her life, with a father who has rejected her since birth and an alcoholic mother who promises to quit drinking but never does. Danielle came to see me, referred by her physician, to learn how to cope with her mother's nearly constant drinking and Danielle's underlying feelings of depression.

Danielle has many strengths and survivor qualities, but her father's rejection and her mother's drinking have left their mark.

"I keep thinking that maybe she'll quit and become more involved in my life. She promises we'll go shopping, but when I come home from school, she's already drunk."

Her alcoholic mother has little understanding of how her addiction causes her to reject her daughter. She has little awareness of the "hole in the soul" she causes her daughter. I provide an outlet for her daughter to grieve, get angry, and share her resentment, but real healing will be slow and a long time coming.

How can Danielle understand her mother's rejection? How does Danielle process her mother's repeated broken promises to quit drinking? How can Danielle deal emotionally with the fact that her father did not care enough about her to remain in her life? These are very troubling issues and will form much of her life's work. She must carve out an identity and a strong self-image through the help of her faith, church family, therapists, and friends.

Abandonment

Even the word *abandonment* sends shivers up our spine. The word evokes images of children sent to foster homes, or in yesteryear or other countries, to orphanages or to live on the streets. Some images are actually true. Abandonment is a far worse fate than transitory rejection. We can process rejection, but abandonment goes to the core of our being.

What do we mean by abandonment? In Danielle's case, her father physically left her, and now she seeks in vain for attention and security from her mother. Other people suffer a crucial loss of connectedness. Abandonment implies the loss of love, feeling thrown away. It involves helpless, dependent children who feel shattered and condemned. Abandonment is the cumulative wound containing all the losses and disconnections of childhood. For many, these losses are severe enough to fracture their entire sense of self.

Feelings of abandonment occur in situations like these:

- A child grieves over the death of her mother.
- A child is permanently discarded by his father.
- A child is emotionally "replaced" by the birth of another child in the family.
- A child feels a sense of isolation within the family.
- A child is abandoned by one parent after the parents' separation and divorce.
- A child feels neglected because of her parents' fighting and violence.
- A child's parents are unavailable emotionally.
- A child feels displaced by his parents' addictions.
- A child feels detached and lost because of her parents' busyness.

Alice Miller, in her book *For Your Own Good,* relates the importance of stability and emotional support for the child.

> Children need a large measure of emotional and physical support from the adult. This support must include the following elements:
>
> 1. respect for the child
> 2. respect for his needs
> 3. tolerance for his feelings
> 4. willingness to learn from his behavior
>   - about the nature of the individual child
>   - about the child in the parents themselves
>   - about the nature of emotional life, which can be observed more clearly in the child than in

the adult because the child can experience
his feelings much more intensely and....un-
disguisedly than the adult.[2]

Children need safety, security, stability, and a sense of belonging. These are basic requirements for raising a healthy child. Many events can occur within a family to make a child feel lost. Cumulative losses can damage the child's self-image. This damaged self-image, or chronic insecurity, can be at the root of many adulthood problems, such as depression, anxiety, and low self-esteem.

Humiliation and Shame

Children have an innate need to feel prized, protected, and admired. They will go to extraordinary lengths seeking this affirmation. Watch any new mother with her child, and you will see this in action. You will see the mother admire the child, the child respond to the mother, and a cyclical response-reaction pattern. The mother adores the child; the child adores the mother. It is a magnificent sight.

Little changes over time. In the early years the child seeks the parent's approval. Feeling safe, secure, and loved, the child will begin to meander away from the parent's sight to explore the world. With a healthy self-image, she takes her "secure self" along with her, knowing all will be right with her world.

But what happens if the child is ridiculed, humiliated, or shamed? What happens if she hears she is bad and should have known better? Bradshaw says shame and humiliation murder a child's soul. "The true self is ruptured and a false self must be created. Shame is a being wound. It says I am flawed as a person."[3]

How do we differentiate guilt from shame? Guilt is a feeling and a state of being stemming from our conscience. It says, "I have failed and must make things right." Shame says, "I not only have done something wrong, but am a bad person and flawed." Shame is a feeling of worthlessness that goes clear to the soul. Nothing the child does can erase her feelings of shame.

Physical and Sexual Abuse

Physical and sexual abuse is, of course, the height of rejection, abandonment, and shame for a child. Any discussion with an abuse survivor will convince you that this severely horrific treatment of a child leads to incredible trauma. Few acts of invasion and betrayal are more egregious.

Children naturally trust adults in their world to treat them respectfully. They enter the world believing it is a safe and loving place. They seek and desperately need adults in their world for protection. When that does not occur, the loss rips through the fabric of a child's feeling of security. She can no longer trust adults to protect her. She is no longer safe.

If a child feels unsafe, and if adults can violate her at their whim, her boundaries are invalidated. She will feel powerless, not only in the present action but for years to come. She may be prone to be violated again and again, physically and emotionally, without secure boundaries. Her life and relationships may feel fragile because she feels a loss of control.

Furthermore, her very worth is at stake. The violated child often believes, *I am not worth anything except what I can give to people. I am a broken, worthless human being. I am flawed down to my core.* This flawed self-image needs a great deal of healing, or it will stay with the child when she is an adult.

Emotional Abuse

Who would dare emotionally abuse their child? How could they? But the cold, hard fact is that we, you and I, are the ones who abuse our children. In fact, the most unsafe place for a child is at home.

Go ahead and take a breath. Tell yourself it cannot be true. Tell yourself you could never emotionally hurt your child. You could never do anything that would impair the psychological growth of a child. The truth of the matter, however, is that you and I can and do hurt our children. We don't set out to hurt them, but it happens.

Statistics reveal that almost any adult involved in a relationship with a child is a potential perpetrator. Parents, teachers, pastors, social workers, and neighbors may all be capable of emotional maltreatment. Any are capable of emotionally abusive behaviors: belittling a child in public, describing a child in negative terms, always assuming a child is at fault, having unrealistic expectations of a child, or threatening a child with severe punishment. What parent has never once withdrawn emotional support or been violent in word or action?

Many experts believe chronic emotional abuse is more damaging to children than physical or sexual abuse. Kids may not have marks or physical scars to show the abuse, but emotional scars run deep and are crippling. Even without physical indicators, behavioral manifestations reveal that things are amiss. Consider the child who exhibits these behaviors:

- acting immature or overly mature
- showing dramatic behavioral changes
- regressing behaviorally, such as by bedwetting or clinging
- being aggressive or antisocial
- having unusual fears
- developing poor relationships with peers
- being unable to react with emotion or develop an emotional bond
- lacking self-confidence

Each of these behaviors suggests emotional problems. Any significant change from one behavior to another is suspicious, and further evaluation of deeper problems may be warranted.

What becomes of a child who is chronically, emotionally abused? The research is clear that emotional abuse is devastating to children, especially to their self-image. They often fail to thrive, and their development is thwarted. Children of emotional abuse can develop lifelong struggles with depression, anxiety, a damaged self-image, inappropriate or troubled adult relationships, lack of empathy, and possible antisocial attitudes and behaviors.

Excessive Expectations

Children inherently attempt to please their parents. They want Mommy and Daddy to be pleased with their accomplishments. Perhaps they intuitively know that their self-worth depends almost completely upon their parents' approval shining down upon them. Parents have an unimaginable amount of power and influence over their children.

Gary Chapman, in his book *The Five Love Languages of Children,* says that words of affirmation and encouragement are vital to a child.

> The word *encourage* means "to instill courage." We are seeking to give children the courage to attempt more. To a young child, almost every experience is new. Learning to walk, to talk, to ride a bicycle requires constant courage. By our words, we either encourage or discourage the child's efforts.[4]

Every new venture requires courage, and children (and adults!) can easily lose courage and become discouraged. This is particularly true when parents have excessive expectations of their children. Excessive expectations provoke anger and discouragement in your child. If your expectations are attainable, your child will be encouraged and even more motivated to please you.

Consider these two examples, spoken by a mother to her seven-year-old daughter:

> "I shouldn't have to remind you to make your bed before going out to play with your friends. You're old enough to never need reminding."

> "I know you can take care of your chores without

> reminding. If you forget, we'll have to think of a plan to
> help you remember."

In the first example the mother uses shame and embarrass-ment to motivate her child. It won't work. She'll invariably resort to scolding her daughter, probably again and again. Parents are destined to frustration when they lower themselves to saying, "You should know better," or "You should never have to be reminded of responsibilities," all the while reminding them!

Am I suggesting we avoid expecting our children to be respon-sible? No, absolutely not. However, I suggest we hold appropriate expectations and set reasonable consequences for any failures.

How do we determine what is right? It is appropriate to have expectations of your child, with the understanding that she may fail to reach them and will need natural consequences. Let's consider the above scene and pretend the child has "forgotten" repeatedly to clean her room. How might an encouraging parent react?

> "Uh-oh!" (Big sigh by parent.) "It looks like you over-looked cleaning your room before inviting your friend over to play. That's too bad—I'm sure you and your friend are going to be disappointed."
> "What do you mean, Mom?"
> "Well, we agreed that if you forgot to clean your room before going out to play, we'd have to come up with a new plan."
> "Yeah, so what does that mean?"
> "Well, I guess you'll have to spend the afternoon cleaning your room. Maybe tomorrow you'll find a way to clean your room before going out to play."

Ouch! Will the little girl scream at the thought of not playing with her friend? Probably so. Will she remember to clean her room tomorrow? Probably so.

Parenting requires balance—especially when parents are practicing Love and Logic techniques we discussed earlier in this book. We must provide boundaries and appropriate expectations for our children. However, those expectations must be appropriate to their age and abilities. If you set the bar too low, your child will not learn self-discipline. If you set it too high, he will become discouraged and give up.

Harsh Punishment

Not long ago I was asked to consult on yet another case of child abuse. Our state's Child Protective Services had been called in at the request of a schoolteacher who noticed red marks across the side of a seven-year-old's face. Upon investigation, social workers found bruising all over the child's body, with especially deep, red welts across her back. The little girl first offered an implausible explanation, stating she had sustained the injuries falling on the playground. Upon further inquiry, she tearfully shared that she had been bad. Her stepfather had used a switch on her back and legs, and he had slapped her when she talked back to him.

The marks and bruising were ghastly to the social workers, but the girl's attitude was even more upsetting.

"I deserved them," she said stoically. "Please don't get mad at my daddy. I disobeyed him and was bad."

I still recoil when I hear stories like this. We falsely comfort ourselves, thinking these are rare occurrences or that they only happen in the dark reaches of the hills of Timbuktu. This is not true. Harsh treatment, meted out in the name of discipline, happens every day in homes of every class. Beatings, given under the euphemism of discipline, happen in many middle-class, Christian homes. In fact, some evidence suggests that Christian parents give harsher, more punitive treatment than do non-Christians.

Being overly harsh in our expectations and discipline of children is very easy. I still vividly recall a horrible evening when my then-16-year-old son Joshua defied my authority. I immediately forgot everything I had learned and taught as a psychologist. I saw red as he stood toe-to-toe with me, daring me to strike him. Rational thought went out the window as I pinned him to the wall and insisted he mind me. In that split second I was out of control. For a moment I was no longer his loving father; he was no longer my delightful son. Tempted to thrust my weight and authority on him, thankfully I backed away and left the room, catching my breath and sanity. But not before injuring the respect my son had for me.

Self-disciplined discipline. This is the mandate of every parent. This is our Hippocratic Oath. We must have a game plan for the expectations we will have for our children, the boundaries we will impose, and the consequences for breaking them.

Gary Chapman, in his book *The Five Signs of a Functional Family*, says every parent must use "creative correction."

> In a functional family, parents give correction when needed. But it is important that correction be given creatively. Remember: our goal is to teach in such a way as to whet the appetite. We want to stimulate the child to positive behavior...Parents often allow their anger to go unchecked and end up with destructive words and behavior. If you feel anger toward your child and believe that the child needs correction, you will do far better to restrain your initial response, give yourself time to cool down, and then come back to verbally correct the child and to give further discipline if needed.[5]

Comparisons

The final concern, which is so damaging to a child's self-image, has to do with comparisons. You might recognize some of the more common comparisons many parents make:

- "Why can't you be as nice as your sister?"

- "Your brother is getting A's. Why can't you?"
- "Everyone else on the team is busting his tail, and all you're doing is sitting around."
- "You should be so much more responsible at your age."
- "All of your friends are nice, but you're mean to them."

At first glance each of these comments may seem reasonable. After all, what's so wrong about telling your son that his sister is nicer? The problem is twofold: First, you are telling your son that he is inferior to his sister. This will not encourage him and is certainly not likely to motivate him to improve his behavior. Second, the comment is shaming—something we know only weakens your child's self-image.

Comparisons can kill. They always have had that kind of power, and they always will. They are dangerous and almost always create turmoil within. Seldom are they helpful to a child's self-image.

The only comparison I have found beneficial is a comparison of current behavior with internally motivated, higher expectations. For example, if Johnny wants to be a better pitcher, he might watch an older athlete and determine to become a better pitcher based upon what he sees this other player doing. If your daughter wants to get into a prestigious college, you might have a discussion with her about how her grades might help her get there.

Parenting Quiz

So, how do you think you are doing as a parent? Did you discover any habits that might harm your child? Take this quiz and see how you fare. Answer them true or false.

1. I am careful to not be overly critical of my   T   F
   child.
2. I allow my child to make mistakes without   T   F
   ridiculing him.

3. Even when busy or tired, I am careful not to push my child away.   T   F

4. I work hard to maintain constancy in my child's life.   T   F

5. I give my child plenty of time and attention.   T   F

6. I am encouraging with my child.   T   F

7. I am careful not to use shaming words with my child.   T   F

8. I allow my child to freely express his emotions.   T   F

9. I guard against my child ever being physically or sexually abused.   T   F

10. I am careful not to emotionally abuse my child.   T   F

11. I maintain appropriate boundaries and expectations for my child.   T   F

12. I negotiate rules with my child.   T   F

13. I am careful not to use harsh punishment with my child.   T   F

14. I hold my child accountable for agreed expectations.   T   F

15. I am careful not to critically compare my child to other children.   T   F

Take a moment and reflect upon your answers. Consider which areas may present difficulty for you and make a decision to work on them.

8

Strengthening
the Family

One hot summer evening during my adolescence, my buddies and I were hiking through the woods toward a private, grassy knoll overlooking the highway, where we often sat and talked about girls, sports, and the turmoils of life—which often included family. As we neared our secret spot, we noticed someone had been here—and left plenty of candy wrappers and beer bottle caps. So much for a private spot! We became suspicious and began looking closer. Suddenly one of my friends saw it—the bounty—cases of beer stacked on top of one another.

We eyed one another in disbelief. How could this be? Could this be a gift from God?

We soon determined that it was probably not a gift from God, and though fortuitous, it meant someone else had discovered our secret hideout and might be back. There was only one reasonable thing to do. Take the beer and transport it to a more private hideout.

We hurriedly found another secret place and began carrying the beer. Halfway through our stealth endeavor, we were confronted by a pair of badge-toting, uniform-wearing gentlemen.

"What are you boys doing with this stolen beer?" they asked.

"Stolen beer?" we stuttered and stammered. "We don't know anything about stolen beer. We just found it up in the woods."

"Found it?" one officer continued in disbelief. "You'll have to come down to the police station and answer some questions."

For the next two hours Mike, Kenny, and I sat in a police office with thoughts of San Quentin running through our minds. As Ricky Ricadro would say, we had some 'splainin' to do.

Thankfully, the truth prevailed. We had not stolen the beer. Thieves had stolen dozens of cases of beer from a nearby beer truck and hidden it in the woods. We were innocent bystanders who just happened upon this liquid gold. Of course, explaining this to our parents was another matter.

My parents were generally reasonable people. However, I had been in some minor trouble before, so my reputation and credibility were a bit tainted. This made my story somewhat incredulous. But in the end, my parents believed me, and another "David story" was written into family lore. My self-image as a relatively honest, relatively law-abiding, relatively good kid was relatively preserved.

As I look back on that situation, it could have turned out very different. The police could have shown up weeks later, after we had time to dip into those cases of beer. Maybe we would have sold the rest—no cost, no overhead, pure profit. My parents could have been far less understanding and easily could have labeled me as a delinquent youth. I could have been placed on probation and caught up in the judicial system. Thank God, none of that happened, and today it is a funny story.

Reflecting on families and the role they play in protecting and preventing problems for children, I reminisce about my parents and my life growing up in a small town in northwest Washington state. I fondly recall my many antics as a child and how I was scolded, challenged, nudged, and generally loved through them into adulthood. My parents and family shielded me from many potential catastrophes that could have propelled me in a very different and dangerous direction.

I am keenly aware of the supportive role my parents and even my siblings played in the development of my self-image. I would be an entirely different person had it not been for my Christian parents, my church family, my siblings, and my neighbors. When Hillary Clinton said it takes a village to raise a child, she was right. It takes at least a village.

It takes a healthy family to grow a healthy child. God knew this when He ordained families. He knew that families would form the fabric of a society that helped children grow into healthy adults. When families break down, children struggle emotionally, physically, and spiritually. When families are strong and have clear convictions and boundaries, children thrive.

Establishing clear convictions and boundaries is no easy task. It means you have considered what kind of family you want to have. It means you have carefully chosen the values you want to impart to your child. It means you have a flight plan before you take off on the journey of parenting.

If you are like I was, you may be halfway to your parenting destination before you consider where exactly you want to end up. If so, don't worry. Most of us are off course 90 percent of the time, yet with thoughtful consideration you can make corrections and turn out just fine. But you do need to stop and think about where you are as a family. Specifically, how are you doing at growing your child's self-image? What needs to change to help you achieve your desired goals?

A Beautiful Family Culture

Let's consider some additional strategies to build a strong, healthy family that can cultivate a healthy self-image in your children.

Steven Covey, author of the immensely popular *The 7 Habits of Highly Effective People,* has also written a book called *The 7 Habits of Highly Effective Families.* In it he writes about the importance of a "beautiful family culture."

> [A family culture is] the chemistry, the climate or atmosphere in the home. It's the character of the family— the depth, quality, and maturity of the relationships. It's the way the family members relate to one another and how they feel about one another. It's the spirit or feeling that grows out of the collective patterns of behavior that characterize family interaction. And these things, like the tip of an iceberg, come out of the unseen mass of shared beliefs and values underneath.[1]

Families are, of course, greater than the sum of their parts. Covey notices a "we" experience that helps define a family. The American culture has long endorsed rugged individualism, but that emphasis may be waning. We have recognized, perhaps a bit too late, that individualism may breed some inner strength, but it promotes loneliness and isolation. The family, especially the Christian family, stands ready to end that era. Members of the Christian family are ready to gain strength from one another and from the larger Christian community.

Establishing a beautiful family culture then is a necessary part of the strengthening of the family. It promotes a "we" culture where we work together for the well-being of each individual. As you consider how to build your child's self-image, the answer will in large part lie in using your energies to build a strong, healthy family. "We" are important—perhaps more important than any "me."

The Importance of Love

Children of all ages need love to enjoy true character development, a cohesive family culture, and a positive self-image. This truth is self-evident. None of us are immune from the desire to love and be loved. Jesus Himself summed up the Jewish law by encouraging us to love God and love others. In the apostle Paul's letter to the Corinthians, he said the greatest gift is love. Nothing compares to this primary family and individual trait. This truth is central to growing children's self-image.

Notice the order of things: Love God and love others. When we love God, everything else will fall into place. We are told to seek first His kingdom, and we will receive everything else we need (Matthew 6:33). Our relationship to the Lord is the source of our love for our children and mates. The apostle John tells us, "We know that we have passed from death to life, because we love our brothers" (1 John 3:14).

Every day I meet with people who protest that they no longer have the feeling of love for another person in the family. A man may no longer feel love for his wife; a wife may have lost that spark for her husband. A parent may be so angry with her son that she feels nothing but spite toward him. What is my counsel? Love! Not the feeling but the action. Love, even when the feelings are not there. Extend yourself sacrificially for another.

How can you love your child when she annoys you? *Love,* the verb, means to listen to your child to see why she might be defiant. *Love,* the verb, means to empathize with your child. Walk in her shoes. Affirm her even when the feeling is not there.

Scott Peck, in his book *The Road Less Traveled,* says, "The desire to love is not love itself…Love is an act of the will—namely an intention and an action. Will also implies choice. We do not have to love." If we are, in spite of good intentions, not loving, it is because we have not chosen to love, Peck suggests. He adds, "On the other hand, whenever we exert ourselves in the cause of spiritual growth, it is because we have chosen to do so. The choice of love has been made."[2]

Why is love so important in the fabric of the healthy family? Stephen Covey suggests that love is the foundation upon which other immensely critical family gifts are built. He notes five gifts that are important aspects of healthy family functioning.

Five Gifts of Healthy Family Functioning

As we consider these five family gifts, I want to share an example from a family who came to me to discuss their "troubled" adolescent. Seth was a 14-year-old youth who, according to his parents, Jim and Cathy Martin, was often angry and disruptive. He picked on his younger brother mercilessly. He sniped at his parents in a disrespectful way. Though he was doing well in school, his behavior within the family was deteriorating. Scolding and yelling at him made little difference, and he seemed to always be grounded. I listened to their plight from the perspective of Covey's five important gifts.

Self-awareness. Covey shares that humans can stand apart from life and observe it with the gift of self-awareness. We can even observe our thoughts. Because of this self-awareness, we can make changes. In counseling I call them "self-corrections."

Our first step in counseling was to stand aside and consider how the family was functioning. Do you have a time when you take stock of how your family is doing? This is a good practice to cultivate in your family.

Every family needs to have a pause button, Covey says. The Martins were ready to push the pause button. Instead of simply reacting emotionally to a situation as it arises, healthy families learn to stand back, reevaluate, and consider what might make better sense. Jim and Cathy decided to stop what they were doing so they could look at its effectiveness.

Conscience. Covey says conscience is another family gift to be developed. Conscience, which of course is a scriptural principle and work of the Holy Spirit, enables you to evaluate family functioning from a moral or ethical perspective. Conscience allows you to evaluate your observations. Do you need to use more discipline with your child? Should you allow greater freedom?

The Martins felt guilty about how they were treating Seth. Often angry with him, they knew they were pushing him away emotionally, doing little to alter his behavior.

Imagination. Covey says a third gift is imagination. The gift of imagination allows us to envision new and exciting possibilities for our child and family. We can look at our past responses and imagine new ones. With the more creative side of your brain you can see how your family is stuck in old ways of behaving and envision new possibilities.

Seth, his parents, and I considered his behavior and how the family might function more effectively. We explored possibilities—what did Seth want to see happen? What did his parents want as an outcome? We used our collective imagination to explore possibilities.

Independent will. You have considered how your family is functioning and have seen the need for change, so you are able to envision new possibilities. Now, with independent will you have the power to take action. With independent will we make choices to better our families. We create a new course of action and begin the process of change. With two-degree changes, small steps, we gradually make very significant progress.

In a family session with Seth, his parents, and his younger brother, Todd, we agreed on some possibilities. Seth wanted more space from his brother, and we arranged this for him. He also wanted more freedom, which we considered in combination with greater responsibility on his part. We also agreed on immediate consequences for angry outbursts, which included apologies to the family. This seemed to alleviate some of the parents' anger at Seth. Most important, we agreed to experiment with these new changes in the family, understanding that they might not work. We would consider more changes if the family continued to struggle.

Sense of humor. Perhaps the most important gift of healthy families is a sense of humor. Covey says a sense of humor is vitally important to the development of a beautiful family culture. The "central element that preserves the sanity, fun, unity, togetherness, and magnetic attraction of our family culture is laughing—telling jokes, seeing the 'funny' side of life, poking holes at stuffed shirts, and simply having fun together."[3]

The Martins, thankfully, had a sense of humor hidden beneath their frustration. They simply needed to rediscover and release it. It was an important element in their healing and the motivation necessary for change.

Consider these five family gifts. How is your family doing? What are your family strengths? Do some areas need attention? You can make a decision to strengthen weak areas.

Purpose and Intention

I have become an expert listener from my years of training and experience. I have learned to tune in to something very important to my clients—their purpose and intention.

Individuals can learn to attend to their purpose and intention—their core values and life direction. What is important to me? What are the changes I want to make to get me where I need to go? What is God saying to me, and how does He want me to change and develop?

Families have their own purpose and intention as well. Healthy families tune in to and develop these subtle aspects of their collective identity. Let's consider how you can use this concept to develop your child's healthy self-image.

Purpose and intention has to do with understanding and following your core values. In family functioning, it is similar to what Dr. Phil McGraw calls "the rhythm of your family life." He says that every phenomenal family has a certain rhythm or beat:

> This is where we're from, this is what we stand for
> and this is what we do together...Life begins with this
> rhythm. An unborn child senses the tympanic sounds
> of his mother's heartbeat in the womb—a calming and

comforting sound that continues after birth…It's this beat of life that provides comfort, the surety and the security that nurtures us and helps us grow, and then connects us to the deeper rhythm of life within our family.[4]

Every individual and family is unique. None of us have the same core values or purpose and intention. Knowing your family's core values is imperative. Consider these questions to help you determine if you are tuned in to your core family values.

- What are the foundational convictions your family lives by all the time?
- Do you talk about these values as a family?
- Do you talk about your family history? Where you came from, your heritage and cultural values?
- Are you clear about family standards of conduct? Do you practice living by them?
- What are your family rituals? How can you reinforce them and make them a stronger part of your family life?

Being clear about your family purpose and intention will help you clarify how you want to raise your children. In fact, self-image and purpose and intention are very similar concepts. For example, our two sons were raised with a number of clear family values:

- We are, first and foremost, a family. We support one another when times are tough.
- We celebrate one another. We laugh, cry, and share emotions together.
- We do not purposely hurt anyone. When we do hurt someone, we take immediate responsibility and make restitution.
- We value honesty, loyalty, faithfulness, sincerity, and generosity.

- We set clear goals and work hard to achieve them.

- We have a Swedish family heritage of which we are proud.

- We are Christians, and we conduct ourselves as such.

- We worship together and belong to a larger Christian community.

These principles do not define the Hawkins family, but they offer a moral, spiritual, and cultural compass for our journey. They are our purpose and intentions. What are yours?

Strong Families and Strong Rituals

Strong, healthy families celebrate rituals. Dr. Phil shares about the power of family rituals in his book *Family First*. He lists four key characteristics that work together so that the ritual takes on special meaning and significance for everyone involved.

Celebration of self. Usually a ritual focuses on a person or persons to express how special they are or to help them identify their unique strengths and qualities. For example, a bedtime ritual of storytelling with your children creates a special bond with them emotionally.

Separation to a sacred or special place. For rituals to be special, they need to take place in a special setting, outside of your regular life. You can do this at your place of worship, go to a special outdoor setting or quiet place, or transform your home environment with candles or music. When I was young my parents used to light a candle and say a prayer with my siblings holding hands when we would leave one another for any significant period of time.

Transition. This part of the ritual acknowledges the person's new role or ushers in a new stage of life. For example, churches offer many rituals that have special meaning, including baby dedications, baptisms, and confirmations. Healthy families often celebrate anniversaries, birthdays, and other events that bring family together.

Personal application to a better life.

> For a ritual to have special meaning, it must allow the individual to connect with and appreciate more than ever what is at the heart of who he or she is. Your child who is given adult status can now have more privileges and more responsibility; or your teenager who has earned an achievement can know he or she has been honored by the family.[5]

The Family of God

I close this book on building your child's self-image with some thoughts about our larger family—the family of God—the church.

It is impossible to talk about strengthening the family without talking about the church. Because of my close connection to the church, I belong to a family larger than my biological one. The church, for all its problems, offers so much. Certainly the writer of Hebrews knew what he was talking about when he said, "Let us not give up meeting together" (Hebrews 10:25).

What does the church mean to me?

Intentionality. The church has always been a powerful place in my psyche. It has been a place where I gather, week in and week out, with others who are intentional about strengthening their spiritual lives. My faith walk has always been different from that of the people sitting next to me in the pew, but I knew they were searching for something, anything that would help deepen their relationship to God. This has been a powerful bond. As I grow older, I care less what the person next to me thinks and believes. That he wants to know God in a deeper, more personal way is enough.

Connection and belonging. I have found few places more significant than the church in my mission to strengthen myself and my family. Others there are intentional about growing stronger in the Lord, so I have an instant connection with them. They are like me in important ways. They want many of the same things I want. This is a mysteriously spiritual place, so we are connected not only in intent and purpose but also in Spirit. The church offers a powerful bond where we can connect to one another as families as much as individuals.

Growth and development. The Scriptures encourage us to grow in the Lord. When the pastor preaches from the Word of God, I am encouraged, admonished, and perhaps convicted. The writer of Hebrews tells us that the Word of God is sharper than any two-edged sword, able to cut deep into our spirit. I need this surgery. My sons need this invasive treatment. My children sat at the knees of countless teachers who nurtured them and helped them develop emotionally and spiritually. My sons have been discipled as have I. The church is a special place of growth.

Protection. Where else can we find a community who cares so deeply about us? Here, in this body of ragamuffins, are folks who are willing to reach out and celebrate with us or walk with us as we grieve. Here, in this body of believers, a circle of friends shields us from many of the dangers of our pagan society. As we are vulnerable and transparent, others with similar issues will form a hedge of protection. This creates a wonderful place for us and our children to grow.

Identity in Christ

Building a strong, healthy family is important to you and your child's health. However, we must be realistic about this matter. At the start of this book we talked about the incredible privilege and opportunity of working in harmony with God in building our children's self-image. As we consider the importance of strengthening your family in order to nurture your child's self-image, we must again remind ourselves that some of the work is ours as parents, but the balance we place in the hands of our Almighty God.

We must remember that our self-image ultimately must be grounded in our identity as children of God. If we get confused about this, we will be heading off in the wrong direction. Our children are part of our immediate family, and our family is part of the larger family of God, but ultimately we belong to Christ Himself. The apostle Paul tells us that "we are God's workmanship, created in Christ Jesus to do good works." How encouraging is that as we approach the challenge of raising healthy children?

Thus, in closing, let's remember that our role as parents is, as Solomon said, to "train up a child in the way he should go so that when he is old he will not depart from it." The way, of course, is to follow Christ. Therefore, my hope is that you will practice the principles found in this book, but more important, that you will follow the principles found in Scripture.

> Fix these words of mine in your hearts and minds; tie them as symbols on your hands and bind them on your foreheads. Teach them to your children, talking about them when you sit at home and when you walk along the road, when you lie down and when you get up (Deuteronomy 11:18-19).

God bless you in this exciting and wonderful journey.

Notes

Chapter 1—Cocreating Our Child's Self-Image

1. Jean Illsley Clark, *Self-Esteem: A Family Affair* (New York: Harper & Row, 1978), 3.

2. Betsy Hart, *It Takes a Parent* (New York: G.P. Putnam's Sons, 2005), 91-92.

3. Bob Murray and Alicia Fortinberry, *Raising an Optimistic Child* (New York: McGraw-Hill, 2006), 104.

4. Ibid.

5. Dorothy Corkille Briggs, *Your Child's Self-Esteem* (New York: Doubleday & Company, 1975), 4.

Chapter 2—The Life of a Child

1. Barbara Coloroso, *Kids Are Worth It* (New York: Collins, 2002).

Chapter 3—How Children Are Made

1. Nathan Ackerman, *The Psychodynamics of Family Life* (New York: Basic Books, 1958), 17.

Chapter 4—The Psychological Needs of a Child

1. Javad Kashani, et al., *Raising Happy Children* (New York: Three Rivers Press, 1998), 59.

2. James Dobson, *The Strong-Willed Child* (Wheaton, IL: Tyndale House Publishers, 1978), 32-33.

Chapter 5—Children and Families Who Struggle

1. www.self-esteem-nase.org

2. M. Covington, "Self-esteem and Failure in School," *The Social Importance of Self-Esteem* (Berkeley: U.C. Press, 1989); L. Lopez, "Keeping Kids Out of Gangs," *Thrust for Educational Leadership,* January, 1992; J. Beane and R. Lipka, *Self-Concept, Self-Esteem, and the Curriculum* (New York: Teacher's College Press, 1984); Rodney Skager, "Prevention of Drug & Alcohol Abuse" (Sacramento: California Attorney General's Office, 1987); J. Battle, *Self-Esteem: The New Revolution* (Edmonton: James Battle and Associates, 1990); H. Piccinini and W.M. Mittic, "Self-Esteem levels of female university students who exhibit bulimic behavior," *Canada's Mental Health,* 35:15-19, 1987.

3. John Bradshaw, *Bradshaw On: The Family* (Deerfield Beach, FL: Health Communications, 1988), 58.

Chapter 6—Building Your Child's Self-Image

1. Edward Hallowell, *The Childhood Roots of Adult Happiness* (New York: Ballantine Books, 2002), 62.

2. Ibid., 63.

3. Ibid., 64.

4. Ibid., 65.

5. Dorothy Corkille Briggs, *Your Child's Self-Esteem* (New York: Doubleday & Company, 1975), 125.

6. Gary and Anne Marie Ezzo, *Growing Kids God's Way* (Chatsworth, CA: Growing Families International Press, 1993), 121.

7. Ibid.

8. Steven Glenn and Jane Nelson, *Raising Self-Reliant Children in a Self-Indulgent World* (Rocklin, CA: Prima Publishing and Communications, 1988), 87.

Chapter 7—Habits That Harm Children's Self-Image

1. John Bradshaw, *Bradshaw On: The Family* (Deerfield Beach, FL: Health Communications, 1988), 144.

2. Alice Miller, *For Your Own Good* (New York: Farrar, Straus, and Giroux, 1990), 72.

3. Bradshaw, 21.

4. Gary Chapman, *The Five Love Languages of Children* (Chicago: Northfield Publishing, 1997), 48.

5. Gary Chapman, *The Five Signs of a Functional Family* (Chicago: Northfield Publishing, 1997), 103.

Chapter 8—Strengthening the Family

1. Stephen Covey, *The 7 Habits of Highly Effective Families* (New York: Golden Books, 1997), 20.

2. M. Scott Peck, *The Road Less Traveled* (New York: Simon & Schuster, 1978), 83.

3. Covey, 33.

4. Phil McGraw, *Family First* (New York: Free Press, 2004), 43.

5. Ibid., 52.

Dr. Hawkins is interested in
hearing about your journey and may be
contacted through his website at
www.YourRelationshipDoctor.com

Other Great Harvest House Books by David Hawkins

(To read sample chapters,
visit www.harvesthousepublishers.com)

When Pleasing Others Is Hurting You

When you begin to forfeit your own God-given calling and identity in an unhealthy desire to please others, you move from servanthood to codependency. This helpful guide can get you back on track.

Saying It So He'll Listen

Dr. Hawkins offers straightforward, intelligent counsel for dealing with sensitive topics in a relationship. You will find new motivation to press through to the goal of effective communication: reconciliation and greater intimacy in marriage.

Nine Critical Mistakes Most Couples Make

Dr. Hawkins shows that complex relational problems usually spring from nine destructive habits couples fall into, and he offers practical suggestions for changing the way husbands and wives relate to each other.

When Trying to Change Him Is Hurting You

Dr. Hawkins offers practical suggestions for women who want to improve the quality of their relationships by helping the men in their lives become healthier and more fun to live with.

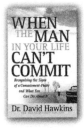

When the Man in Your Life Can't Commit

With empathy and insight Dr. Hawkins uncovers the telltale signs of commitment failure, why the problem exists, and how you can respond to create a life with the commitment-phobic man you love.

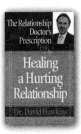

The Relationship Doctor's Prescription for Healing a Hurting Relationship

Dr. Hawkins uncovers the hidden reasons why you may be hurting emotionally. He offers practical steps you can take to heal your hurt and suggests a plan for preventing needless pain in the future.

The Relationship Doctor's Prescription for Living Beyond Guilt

Dr. Hawkins explains the difference between real guilt, false guilt, shame, and conviction, bringing these feelings into the light and demonstrating how they can reveal the true causes of emotional pain.